Liverpool: A

By the same author

Tank Tracks to Rangoon - The Story of British Armour in Burma
A History of Blitzkrieg
Knights of the Black Cross - Hitler's Panzerwaffe and Its Leaders
Desert Warfare
The Czar's British Squadron *(with Anthony Lord)*
Encyclopaedia of the Second World War *(with Ian Hogg)*
Last Stand – Famous Battles Against the Odds
At All Costs –Stories of Impossible Victories
Against All Odds – Dramatic Last Stand Actions
Impossible Victories – Ten Unlikely Battlefield Successes
Seize and Hold – Master Strokes on the Battlefield
Iron Fist – Classic Armoured Warfare Case Studies
The Battle Book – Crucial Conflicts in History from 1469 BC to the Present
The Real Hornblower – The Life and Times of Admiral Sir James Gordon, GCB
Gunboat – Small Ships at War
Heroes of the Hour – Brief Moments of Military Glory
The Taste of Battle – Front Line Action 1914 - 1991
For Valour – Victoria Cross and Medal of Honour Battles

LIVERPOOL

A City at War

Bryan Perrett

HUGO PRESS LIMITED

First published in Great Britain 1990
Reprinted in Great Britain 2005

Hugo Press Limited
7 Maple Avenue
Burscough
Lancashire

British Library Cataloguing in Publication Data

Perrett, Bryan,1934–
Liverpool: a city at war.
1. Merseyside (Metropolitan County). Liverpool, 1936 - 1945
I. Title
942.7'5308

ISBN 0-9550324-0-7

Typeset & Printed in Great Britain by
Rufford Printing Company, Mawdesley, Lancashire L40 3TE

Contents

Acknowledgments

I should like to offer my sincere thanks to the following for their patience, kindness, encouragement and generous assistance: Eric Stokes and Colin Hunt of the *Liverpool Post and Echo* Group: Mr Norman Kinghorn; Mr John D. Robertson and the Merseyside Fire Brigade; Mr David Ryan of the Maritime Records Centre, Merseyside Maritime Museum; Miss Margaret Procter and Mr R.J. Devanny of the Merseyside Residuary Body; Liverpool Central Libraries; Lancashire Library; the Historical Section, Naval Staff Duties, Ministry of Defence; the Royal Artillery Institution; the Air Historical Branch, Ministry of Defence; the Royal Air Force Museum, Hendon; the Museum and Historical Research Section, Bank of England; the National Railway Museum, York; and the Institution of Civil Engineers.

Bryan Perrett
June 1989

Illustrations

PICTURE CREDITS

Merseyside Residuary Body: 1, 2, 3, 13, 14, 20; *Liverpool Daily Post & Echo:* 4, 5, 8, 9, 10, 15, 16, 17, 19, 20, 22, 23; Stewart Bale Collection, Archives Department: 6, 18; Merseyside Fire Brigade: 7,11,12.

Every effort has been made to trace the heirs of the artist George Grainger Smith (*The Enemy Raid* - jacket picture). The publishers would be pleased to hear from readers who can offer any assistance.

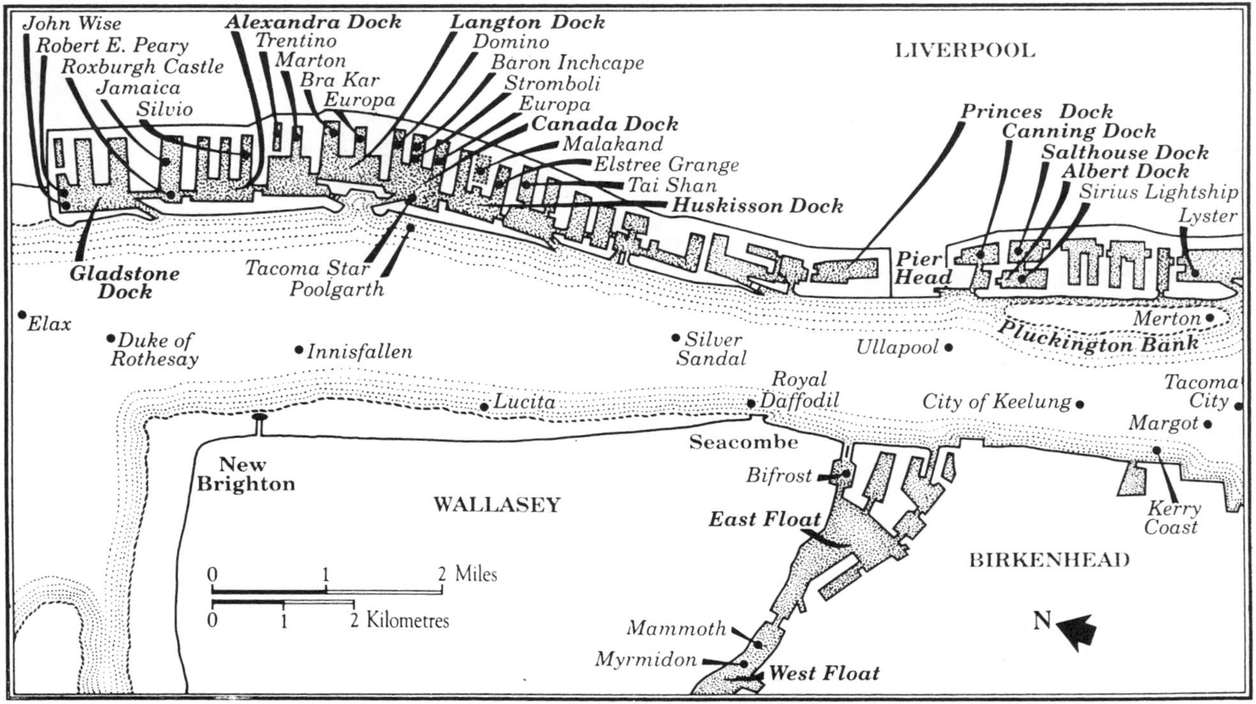

Marine casualties in the docks and river. 1939/41

Marine casualties in the area of the Bar Lightship and the approaches to the Mersey, 1939/41

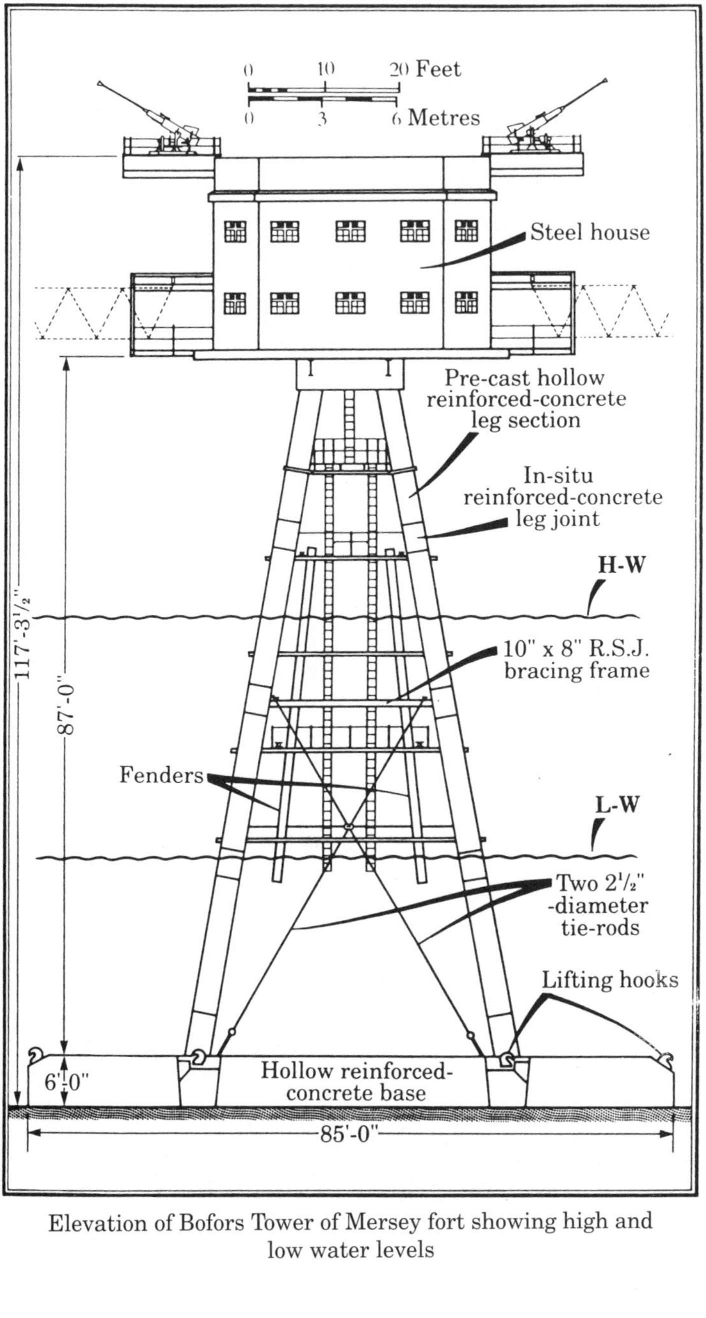

Elevation of Bofors Tower of Mersey fort showing high and low water levels

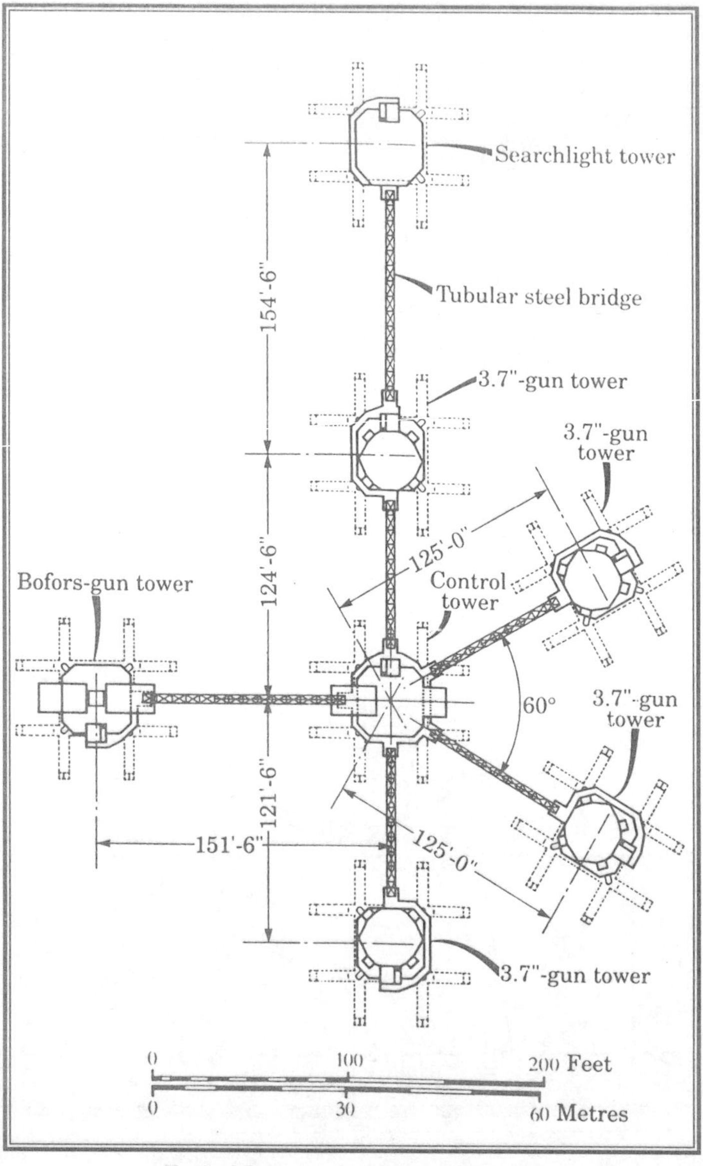

Typical Layout of a Maunsell sea fort

Introduction

From Peace to War

No one wanted it, but now it was inevitable. The days of appeasement were over, although Adolf Hitler refused to recognize the fact and was hell-bent on invading Poland, despite the guarantees given to the Polish government by the United Kingdom and France. Once again, as in 1914, the world was heading for the brink of catastrophe at a pace which the techniques of crisis management seemed unable to control. The probability of war had become a certainty, the only unanswered question being when.

All over the country reservists were reporting to their depots and the recently doubled Territorial Army was mobilized. Some Territorial units were already embodied, having reported for their fortnight's annual training little realizing that it would be six years before they wore civilian clothes again. Everywhere, families gathered outside drill halls to see off their men. Sometimes, the natural anxieties of parting were relieved by unexpected humour. At the drill hall in Park Street, Bootle, the headquarters of the 40th Royal Tank Regiment (TA), it was said that only the commanding officer and the caretaker's wife knew the War Office's plans for the unit. 'Don't worry, lads,' shouted the latter as the men tumbled into their lorries, 'You're only going to Crosby!' And so they were, for the moment. After that, their travels would take them to El Alamein, across

North Africa to Tunisia, then to Salerno, the Garigliano and Cassino, and finally to Greece to intervene in a bloody civil war. Along the way, they became known as Monty's Foxhounds and were the only unit ever to bear the Field Marshal's name.

In 1939 precautions were taken which had not been necessary in 1914. Then, the sea had served as a moat which protected Great Britain from the wrath of her enemy; now, that same enemy possessed fleets of bomber aircraft which were capable of unleashing destruction on the nation's cities, just as they had on the little town of Guernica during the Spanish Civil War. Everyone was concerned by the prospect of air attack, and in particular by the possibility of being attacked with poison gas, which the enemy had not shrunk from using during what was now called the Great War. Gas masks were already being issued and on 31 August 1939 the process began of evacuating tens of thousands of children from the cities to safer rural areas. The following day the German Army invaded Poland at 04:45. The British and French governments promptly demanded its withdrawal and on 2 September issued an ultimatum which few imagined would be answered.

Like every city, town and village in the land, Liverpool contained very few families which tragedy had not touched in some way during the Great War. The names of its lost generation of soldiers, sailors, airmen and merchant seamen were recorded on memorials and plaques in churches, offices and factories throughout the city. Annually, at eleven o'clock on 11 November, the hour of Armistice, the sounds of Liverpool would be reduced to silence for two minutes, whatever the day of the week. Traffic would stop of its own accord, or be halted by the police. On the pavements, in business premises, homes and schools, all movement would cease. Men removed their hats in respect for fallen comrades and women wept quietly for the fathers, sons, brothers, husbands and lovers who never returned. Sharing in the silence, too, were the many who had returned crippled or eyeless, or with their nerves shattered beyond repair by their experiences, or their lungs rotted by gas. The city's collective grief was enshrined in a cenotaph on St George's Plateau, unveiled by the Earl of Derby on Armistice Day, 1930. Regrettably, and despite its superb architectural setting, it consisted of nothing more than an ugly, monolithic catafalque which offered neither grace nor comfort to the bereaved, but merely the fact of physical death.

On 2 September 1939, therefore, there was none of the enthusiasm for war which had been evident in 1914. Rather, there was the profoundest sadness that the whole horrible ordeal had to be repeated. Equally, there was a quiet but equally intense anger induced by the nature of Nazism, and a general recognition that, sooner or later, an evil of this magnitude would have to be confronted and crushed if a lasting peace was to be attained. If the moment had come, it was unwelcome, but so be it.

Understandably, the *Liverpool Echo* was preoccupied with the day's major events. It provided such details as were available of the fighting in Poland, as well as articles on the progress of evacuation and mobilization. In his speech to the Reichstag, Hitler had given a categorical assurance that he had no intention of waging war on women and children; few believed him, and the editor certainly did not, since nearby were some hints on how to tackle an incendiary bomb. Among the shipping movements recorded was the departure of the Donaldson Atlantic Line's 13,465-ton *Athenia*, commanded by Captain James Cook, bound for Montreal, with 1,417 passengers aboard, including some 300 Americans anxious to escape the impending war in Europe. Blackler's department store, appreciating that hard times lay ahead, offered a wide variety of goods at half price, including men's worsted suits at 45/- (£2.25p), ladies' swagger coats at 20/- (£1), nightgowns at 2/9d (13p), stockings at 9½d (4p) a pair, and kitchen cabinets at 59/6d (£2.97p). Of greater interest to younger readers were the continuing adventures of Curly Wee and Gussie Goose, an intrepid pair so popular that the porcine partner would have a Grant tank named after him by its Liverpool crew in the Western Desert. If one wished to escape from the reality of this, the last Saturday of peace, Shirley Temple was starring in *The Little Princess* at the Trocadero, while across London Road at the Paramount (now the Odeon), Irene Dunne and Charles Boyer provided romance in *Love Affair;* the Paramount also showed trailers of its next programme, *Beau Geste,* with Gary Cooper, Ray Milland and Robert Preston. There were, of course, many other cinemas both in the city and the suburbs, and for live entertainment the Empire, Royal Court, Playhouse, Shakespeare, Pavilion and Rotunda theatres offered a wide variety of programmes ranging from drama to vaudeville. At the Grafton Rooms, which possessed one of the best sprung floors in the country, there was ballroom dancing. For most people, however, the evening was a thoughtful one. If they did not stay at home they went for a quiet drink at their local; in both places the focus of attention was the radio and its periodic news bulletins.

The following morning dawned fine, bright and warm. There were the usual Sunday sounds of church bells and distant bands belonging to the Salvation Army, the Boys' Brigade, the Boy Scouts or the Orange Order. In those days, church-going was more commonplace and the best-attended service of the day was Evensong. On 3 September, however, there were many fresh faces at Matins, each with their hopes and fears to express as best they could. At 11.15 the Prime Minister, Neville Chamberlain, broadcast to the nation. He said that on 1 September the British Ambassador in Berlin had informed the German Government that unless it was: prepared to give assurance that aggressive actions against Poland would be suspended, and that German troops would be withdrawn from Polish territory, the: United Kingdom would fulfil its obligations. At 9 a.m. this morning, the Prime Minister continued, the British Ambassador had informed the German Foreign Minister, Herr von Ribbentrop, that unless, not later than 11 a.m. (British Summer Time), 3 September, such assurances were received, a state of war would exist between the two countries from that hour. No such undertaking had been received, and the country was now at war. Pausing briefly to allow his words to sink in, Chamberlain concluded, slowly and with infinite sorrow in his voice: 'Now may God bless you all. May we defend the right. It is evil things that we shall be fighting against – brute force, bad faith, injustice, oppression and persecution, and against them I am certain that the right will prevail.'

No one spoke. There was nothing to say, and after a while the women returned to preparing the Sunday lunch, and the men to whatever they had been doing before the broadcast; some made their way to the recruiting offices. Some fifteen minutes after the Prime Minister had finished speaking there was the sound of gunfire from the river. Used to the punctual daily bang of the One o' Clock Gun, people glanced at their watches in surprise. These, the first shots of the war, were fired by Captain C.J. Cocks, commanding the coast defence artillery battery at Fort Perch Rock, who had put two rounds across the bows of a vessel illegally attempting to enter the now closed Rock Channel approach to the Mersey. It was good to have so prompt a demonstration that the armed services were doing their job.

That afternoon, for the first time in its history, the *Liverpool Echo* appeared on a Sunday, abandoning its traditional front-page format of small-print advertisements in favour of banner headlines reporting the declaration of war and announcing that the King was to broadcast at six o'clock. The stop press contained details of the recently received German response to the British ultimatum which, predictably, was rejected in arrogant and derisive terms. Also reported was the Government's temporary decision to close all theatres and cinemas, and to prohibit sports meetings, until further notice. With immediate effect, the frequency of the Liverpool tram service was to be reduced after sunset, and from 10.30 p.m. a skeleton service only would operate on the main routes.

During the evening, Liverpool sustained its first

casualties. By now, the *Athenia* was 250 miles north-west of Ireland. News of the British declaration of war had been picked up by the ship's radio and at noon was communicated to the passengers by Captain Cook, who reassured them that they were protected by international law. Nevertheless, the ship was blacked out and a zigzag westward course was set. The German Navy, in fact, had already despatched much of its U-boat fleet to its war stations some days earlier and at approximately 7.30 p.m. the *Athenia* was sighted by U-30, commanded by a 26-year-old regular officer, Lieutenant Fritz-Julius Lemp. At 7.35 p.m three torpedoes were fired at the darkened ship, one of which exploded amidships on the port side, inflicting a mortal wound. As the passengers and crew took to the boats *Athenia* transmitted a coded distress call, reporting her position and the fact that she had been torpedoed by a submarine. In an attempt to stop the transmissions Lemp surfaced and opened fire with his deck gun. By now, the *Athenia* was settling and Cook had switched on the ship's lights to assist the lowering of the boats Horrified by the discovery that, contrary to specific orders, he had sunk a passenger liner, Lemp ceased firing and submerged. Other vessels, including three warships, began converging on the scene and, together, these picked up the survivors, but 118 passengers and crew, of whom eighty-five were women and children, had lost their lives.

For Germany, the *Athenia* affair was an unmitigated disaster. At first, Dr Josef Goebbels, the Minister of Propaganda, could only offer the suggestion that the liner had been sunk in error by a British warship or a British mine, but he quickly recovered his balance and by 22 September was alleging that Winston Churchill, then First Lord of the Admiralty, had himself ordered the ship to be sunk in order to discredit Germany. When U-30 returned home, Lemp and his crew were sworn to secrecy and all trace of the sinking was removed from the submarine's log. Lemp himself was genuinely shaken by the enormity of his mistake and did his best to make amends. On 11 September he sank the freighter *Blairlogie* but stayed with the lifeboats, firing distress flares until a neutral American ship arrived. Three days later he sank a second freighter, the *Fanad Head,* and was actually towing her boats towards the Irish coast when he was attacked by aircraft of the Fleet Air Arm and forced to cast off his charges and dive. Fate had a strange way of paying her debts, and in May 1941, the month in which Liverpool underwent the most savage ordeal in its history, Lemp was again to be the principal actor in a drama which resulted in dire consequences for the Third Reich.

The facts relating to the sinking of the *Athenia* did not become public knowledge until the war had ended. At the time, comparison could hardly be avoided between her loss and the murderous attack on the *Lusitania* in May 1915; there were, too, seamen aboard the *Athenia* who had been torpedoed during the earlier conflict. For the wrong reasons, the correct conclusion was reached that against so ruthless an enemy there could only be war to the death, until the matter was resolved once and for all.

The outbreak of World War II placed Liverpool in a position of immense strategic importance. After London, it was the United Kingdom's largest port, as well as being the major port closest to the Americas. In 1939, in addition to being a busy centre for coastal traffic, it handled almost one-third of the nation's imports and exports. This proportion was bound to rise sharply in view of the vulnerability of London and the east coast ports to air attack, mining, U-boats and the enemy's coastal forces. It was not forgotten that during a critical period of World War I, the German submarine offensive had reduced the country's food stocks to a mere six weeks' supply. In 1939, the United Kingdom imported half its food and although it was calculated that it could manage if food imports were themselves reduced by half, the import of the raw materials and weapons needed to wage war, and the waging of war itself, depended on keeping the ocean lifelines open. Equally important was the need to preserve the means of handling and distributing these goods once they reached harbour, since without these facilities the entire effort of the war at sea was wasted. At one period the Luftwaffe undoubtedly possessed the ability to destroy Liverpool and its port. If it had done so the effect, combined with the more distant U-boat attacks on the sealanes, would have been decisively to weaken the United Kingdom to the point that history would probably have taken a number of different courses. For example, the final victory in North Africa would have been delayed and the collapse of Italy averted indefinitely; and Operation Bolero, the transatlantic shipment of troops and equipment for the Allied invasion of Europe, would have taken far longer to complete, with the result that D-Day might have been delayed for almost a year, with incalculable consequences. If, on the other hand, the port could be kept operating, ultimate victory was probable, particularly after the United States entered the war.

What took place in Liverpool between 1939 and 1945, therefore, was a battle of importance comparable to any fought during the war, and as with every battle, it is necessary to consider the ground over which it was fought, the strength and weakness of the combatants, their plans, actions and errors, before it can be fully understood. Above all, it is necessary to understand the nature of Liverpool itself and of its population, since both are unlike any other in the country. In recent years, it has been fashionable for television producers to show Liverpudlians as a series of unattractive stereotypes; in fact, such stereotypes exist in every city, and they do not win battles. The people amongst whom I grew up during these, some of the most exciting years of my life, were the precise antithesis of such individuals. They possessed a fierce independence, a product of their history, which was never less than vigorous, and often violent. They were also kindly, understanding, good-humoured and hardworking, fiercely loyal to their families, their street and the area of the wider community in which they lived. They set immense store on fair play, in every aspect of their lives. They loved a good story and took merciless delight in puncturing pomposity or pretence. Totally unimpressed by power, wealth and education, they would assess strangers as equals, and, if they approved, treat them with astounding generosity. Bad leadership they despised, and said as much. Good leadership they recognized and responded to; well led, they made fine soldiers and superb seamen. Fifty years on, they are the same people, and this is the story of their war, as much as my own.

1

Second City of Empire

For centuries there was no such place as Liverpool. Perhaps the narrow, mud-fringed coastal strip on the eastern shore of the Mersey, backed by a low ridge of rolling sandstone hills, may once have had a local name, but if so it has gone beyond recall. Few went there, since the fast-flowing tidal estuary was difficult to cross, while to the north and east it was isolated from the mainstream of national life by a wide belt of swamp and forest. It is said that St Patrick sailed to Ireland from the Mersey in the year AD 432, but beyond this tradition little occurred that was worth recording. After the Norman Conquest the area was given to Roger of Poitiers, who commenced building a castle there in 1073. There is no mention of Liverpool in the Domesday Book, although there are entries for Everton and other nearby villages. The first reference to Liverpool occurs in 1089, by which time a small community of farmers and fishermen had begun to develop around the protection afforded by the castle. By 1112 this had expanded sufficiently for Henry I to grant the town the first of its numerous charters. Essentially, however, Liverpool remained little more than a village, bounded by the Mersey on one side and on the other by the Pool, an inlet south of the modern

Pier Head, winding its way to the foot of the ridge along the line of present-day Paradise Street and Whitechapel; this, legend has it, was the haunt of the Liver Bird. Across the Mersey, a similar inlet penetrated deep into the Wirral peninsula, separating Birkenhead (the birch wood on the headland) from Wallasey (the island of the Welsh), the place names in themselves confirming the relentless pressure imposed on the indigenous Celtic population by successive waves of invaders during the previous centuries.

Throughout the Middle Ages, and well beyond, Liverpool formed part of the Hundred of West Derby and was only granted corporate status in the reign of Charles I. Similarly, the town lay within the parish of Walton and did not become a parish in its own right until 1699. In medieval times it had no status as a maritime centre and was described simply as 'a creek of the port of Chester'. However, some ships were using the river and in 1338 Edward III required the town to provide a small vessel and six sailors for service in his French wars. Because of its isolation, Liverpool might have hoped to escape the Black Death, but the plague arrived with visitors and such were its effects that permission was given for the dead to be buried in the surrounding countryside. By and large, however, the town remained immersed in its internal affairs. In 1424 it came close to being a battleground when Sir Richard Molyneux and Sir Thomas Stanley, forebears respectively of the Earls of Sefton and Derby, each collected 2,000 men and proposed settling their differences by force; they were only prevented from doing so by the timely arrival of the Sheriff's messenger from Lancaster, armed with the King's writ.

Meanwhile, the sea itself, with infinite slowness, was creating the conditions which would make Liverpool's fortune. On the other side of the Wirral peninsula lay the estuary of the River Dee, through which passed shipping bound for Chester, then the principal port for Ireland. The Dee, however, became progressively narrower as it passed between the Wirral and the Welsh coast and, year by year, its upper reaches silted to the point at which only small vessels could reach Chester. The Mersey, on the other hand, after passing through a narrow channel, broadened into a wide, inland tidal lake, resembling a bottle with a narrow neck. Twice a day tides filled and emptied the lake, surging past Liverpool and through the narrows in a dangerous race which nevertheless created sufficient scour to keep a deep-water channel open. In such circumstances the decline of Chester as a port could only be of benefit to Liverpool. During the latter half of the sixteenth century there were, as today, troubles in Ulster and, significantly, it was from Liverpool that troops were despatched to contain the rebellion. It is recorded that in 1573 the town was 'much pestered and charged with soldiers going to Ireland, and many disturbances created by the military'. That same year the passengers and crew of a Liverpool ship stranded near Carrickfergus were murdered by the rebels.

During the English Civil War the town was garrisoned by Parliamentary troops and fortified by an earth rampart running along the inner shore of the Pool and thence back to the Mersey. Despite the fact that Prince Rupert regarded the defences with derision, declaring that Liverpool was 'a crow's nest a parcel of boys might take', it took him twenty-four days to capture it. The final assault was launched against the weakest sector of the defences, in the area of Old Hall Street, on 26 June 1644, and, driven back, the garrison surrendered near the Town Hall. The damage inflicted must have been considerable for, following Rupert's own defeat at Marston Moor and the return of Parliamentary troops, Parliament granted compensation of £10,000 and 500 tons of timber, to be taken from the estates of the Earl of Derby, Lord Molyneux, and other local Royalists.

By the time the Civil War ended Liverpool had overtaken Chester, owning twenty-four ships amounting to 462 tons, against the latter's fifteen ships of 383 tons. Both the number of ships and the size of the town continued to grow slowly but steadily until by the year

1700 it contained approximately 5,000 inhabitants. The next century witnessed such an explosion of commercial activity that by 1751 the population had risen to 18,000, and by 1800 to 80,000.

The earliest cargoes reaching Liverpool had included wine, Irish linen and, from the 1640s, tobacco. During the eighteenth century trade with Ireland, the Americas and the West Indies increased rapidly. Major imports included sugar, rum, tropical fruits, tea, coffee, cocoa, timber and, later, cotton. Exports included salt, coal, pottery, tools, cutlery and general goods. Even at this stage Liverpool did nothing by halves, and recognizing the difficulties involved in handling cargo in the fast-flowing estuary, enclosed the Pool to create the first commercial wet dock in the world, opened in 1715. This, known as the Old Dock, was the first of many Liverpool superlatives during the next 250 years, and coincided with the publication of the world's first provincial newspaper, *The Liverpool Courant*. The dock's facilities, however, were clearly unable to cope with the huge expansion of trade and in 1753 it was joined by the Salthouse Dock, then two dry docks in 1765, followed by George's Dock in 1771, King's Dock in 1788 and Queen's Dock in 1796. These facilities were backed by extensive warehouses of which the best-known example, the Goree, survived until the late 1940s.

During this period, too, the first steps were taken to establish the port's superb transportation infrastructure. Bulk cargoes such as coal, salt and pottery were difficult to transport along the primitive road system of the period, but conveyance by water to the Mersey from the production centres inland provided an obvious alternative. The upper reaches of the Mersey itself, the Irwell and the Weaver were all put into a navigable state and canals were cut where no rivers existed. The Duke of Bridgewater's Canal reached Runcorn in 1773 and the following year the Leeds and Liverpool Canal was opened as far as Wigan. This led to the construction of the small Duke's and Manchester Docks, owned respectively by the Duke of Bridgewater and the Mersey and Irwell

Navigation Company, which were used by the companies' sailing barges, known locally as flats.

By the end of the century Liverpool was rich, and becoming steadily richer. General shipping business produced most of the town's wealth, although there were other routes to affluence. For a while, Liverpool was a whaling port. Whalemen were exempt from the Royal Navy's hated press, and the following incident serves to emphasize Liverpool's sense of playing by the rules and resentment of outside interference. In July 1759 His Majesty's 26-gun ship *Vengeance* was lying off the mouth of the Mersey, making up her numbers from the crews of passing vessels. One of those stopped was the whaler *Golden Lyon,* homeward bound from the Greenland fisheries. A lieutenant sent across to empress some of her men received a rough reception and was tossed over the side into his boat, and the *Golden Lyon* continued upriver. Enraged, the captain of the *Vengeance* set off in pursuit, opening fire with his bow-chasers. Little damage was done to the whaler, but several balls smacked into buildings in the town. It was now the turn of the civil authorities to be outraged, but worse was to follow. The *Golden Lyon's* men hurried ashore and headed straight for the Customs House to renew their exemption certificates, and in hot pursuit came an armed landing party from the *Vengeance.* Inside the Customs House a full-scale brawl ensued in which pistol shots were fired. While the fighting raged around several magistrates who had been attempting to attend to their private commercial interests, a crowd gathered and assisted most of the whalemen to get safely away, but their skipper, Captain Thomson, and five of his crew, were marched off in triumph to the warship. Their dignity ruffled, the magistrates threatened the officers of the *Vengeance* with the full weight of the law. The Navy was not impressed, pointing out tartly that a King's officer had been assaulted and that the magistrates themselves had failed to prevent the townsmen from interfering illegally with the activities of the press gang. As a sop to wounded pride Thomson was set ashore, but there the matter ended.

Another, and more violent, road to riches was privateering. This involved private citizens fitting out vessels at their own expense to prey upon the commerce of the King's enemies. To add some semblance of respectability to what was in fact a form of licensed piracy, letters of marque had to be obtained, but such letters were issued without question at the Post Office on payment of a few shillings. Many merchant vessels carried letters of marque as a matter of course on the chance that they might pick up a prize or two during the normal run of business, but more often the bearers were ships that had been designed specifically for commerce raiding. The ideal privateer was small, fast, handy, mounted between ten and thirty guns, usually twelve-pounders, and, in the words of one professional privateersman, should 'look as little and defenceless as possible and conceal her power till there is real occasion for it, and then as suddenly as possible to give the greater surprise'. She carried a very large crew for her size, including a number of landsmen whose function was to provide boarding parties. Officers and men were tough and many of the latter came from the town's criminal element who had joined to escape the press gang or the magistrates. Discipline was enforced with fists, the rope's end and the club.

The object of the privateer was not to batter her prey into surrender, but to get close enough to disable her. Often this was enough to ensure that the enemy struck his colours, but if it was not the boarders would be sent over with pike, cutlass, blunderbuss and pistol to finish the job. A prize crew would be put in charge of the captured vessel, which was then sailed to the nearest friendly port, where she and her cargo would be sold. Occasionally, if the prize was a good ship, she would be sent back to Liverpool. Of course, it was not all plain sailing. Sometimes the privateer would get the worst of the engagement or, worse, fall in with an enemy warship or privateer. The prospect of pulling an oar in a French or Spanish galley, or sweating the years away in a Barbary gaol, cannot have been a pleasant one. Notwithstanding, there were fortunes to be made from privateering and there was never a lack of subscribers willing to equip a suitable vessel. The first recorded Liverpool privateer was the *Relief,* which was at sea during Queen Elizabeth I's Spanish wars. The practice reached its height during the eighteenth century when, between 1777 and 1783, no fewer than 120 privateers were fitted out in Liverpool; in 1779 these earned a total of over £1 million for their shareholders. The largest return was made by the *Mentor,* a 28-gun vessel commanded by Captain John Dawson and owned by Baker and Company. On 28 October 1778 the *Mentor* captured the *Carnatic,* a French East Indiaman with a total cargo value of £170,000 and a box of diamonds worth £135,000 aboard. The proceeds enabled Dawson to marry Baker's daughter, and Baker built himself a fine mansion on fashionable Mossley Hill, naming it Carnatic Hall. Another elegant dwelling built with the rewards of privateering was San Domingo, situated on the ridge near Everton, named after the French West Indian island near which the plunder had been acquired.

Liverpool privateers were out again during the Napoleonic Wars, but the long spell of peace which followed Waterloo spelled the end of the professional privateersman, whose career was formally ended by an international treaty in 1856, the terms of which forbade the use of private vessels as instruments of war. In Liverpool, however, ingrained habits took a long time to die. The town had a long and profitable business association with the southern states of America and was sympathetic to the Confederacy when civil war broke out. As a result, Liverpool became a hotbed of espionage with the United States Consul, Thomas H. Dudley, and the Confederate agent, James D. Bulloch, maintaining a watch on each other's activities from their respective offices in Tower Buildings and Rumford Street. Using transparently thin cover stories, Bulloch arranged for two commerce raiders, the *Florida* and the *Alabama,* to be built locally and when these left the Mersey in 1862 they did so with Liverpool crews. So destructive were their cruises that Great Britain was forced to pay the United States £3 million in compensation. Nor was this Liverpool's only maritime contribution to the Confederate cause. Fast ships were built to run the Union blockade of the South, and these earned generous profits for their owners.

Perhaps the best known of Liverpool's eighteenth-century business activities was the infamous African Trade, which was simply a euphemism for slaving. This involved what was known as the Triple Passage, on the first leg of which ships would carry simple trading goods such as pots, pans, mirrors, beads, cotton cloth, old muskets and whatever their captains considered that their African associates in the Bight of Benin (then called Bonny) would take a fancy to; at one time four-poster beds were in great demand as status symbols. At Bonny, the trash goods would be handed over to the slave catchers, with a cash or barter adjustment either way, and the slaves would be crammed aboard, heavily manacled, and chained down head to tail until there was not an inch of space left between decks. The ships, known as Blackbirders, were built for speed but even so the term is relative and a percentage of the human cargo always died, sometimes from sheer terror; this the captains regretted sincerely, since every death reduced their own personal share of the profit. Decent seamen refused to serve aboard the slave ships and it was said that, once smelled, the stench of a Blackbirder was never forgotten.

The slaves were shipped to the southern American colonies, as they were for much of the century, to South America, and to the West Indies. There they were sold by lot to the highest bidder, the best prices being obtained in the West Indies, which required a vast number to work the sugar plantations in a climate rife with tropical diseases often fatal to Europeans. The death rate on the plantations was high, partly because of overwork and partly because, for their part, the slaves had no resistance to European diseases; the demand for replacements was constant.

For the final, homeward, leg of the voyage, some of the funds accumulated from the sale of the slaves would be used to purchase cargoes of sugar, coffee, ginger, spices, tobacco and raw cotton, all of which could be sold profitably on arrival. An astute captain could produce a profit at every phase of the operation. A few individual slaves did reach Liverpool; on 23 August 1767 three young male slaves were offered at an auction, and on 1 December one negro man and two boys were advertised as being for sale at the office of a Mr Robinson. These were among the last of such transactions, for from 1772 onwards a slave became a freeman as soon as he reached the United Kingdom. Nevertheless, second, third or fourth generation plantation hands of both sexes continued to be shipped to Liverpool at a discreet premium paid by fashionable members of society who enjoyed displaying their wealth in the form of negro footmen, maids, train-bearers and fan-holders.

Liverpool joined the African Trade in 1700, long after London and Bristol, but from 1750 onwards dominated the field to such an extent that its ships carried as many slaves as those of all other ports, British and European, put together. It has been calculated that at the height of the African Trade some £1,120,000 was remitted annually to Liverpool from the West Indies alone, producing a net profit of £215,000, excluding profits earned from the sale of cargoes in the home port. In general, however, the business tended to run at a steady eight per cent profit, total and occasional trading losses being balanced by better than average results.

Slaving accounted for only one-tenth of the town's maritime business, but it was supported by a very vocal lobby which for years was able to keep the Abolitionists at bay. The slavers' argument was that no one knew what was in the Almighty's mind when he created Africa, but it was a dreadful place in which people were compelled to live in ignorance and at the mercy of their neighbours; and that being the case, it was the bounden duty of good men to rescue them from their misery by shipping them to plantations where they could be introduced to the benefits of a Christian lifestyle and given some education; furthermore, the port would be ruined if the trade were stopped. Not even its authors really believed this cynical claptrap, and for generations after the African Trade had ended any mention of the subject was socially taboo in the town's society. Yet, if Liverpool played a leading role in this horrible business and, as was said at the time, 'every brick in the town is cemented with an African's blood', it was also Liverpool men who were responsible for obtaining its abolition in 1807.

At this period Liverpool contained more elegant Georgian houses than Bath, grouped in terraces and squares, many of which still exist. There were also a number of good if rather plain churches, built in the style of Wren. There were shops to serve every need, a theatre, a concert hall, a library, several banks, and a cross-section of hotels and inns. Much business was still conducted in coffee houses, but the hub of commercial activity was the Exchange, where ship-owners, merchants, agents and underwriters met daily. Surprisingly, for a town which had once unceremoniously packed off its beggars to Barbados and was still deeply immersed in the African Trade, there were also numerous philanthropic institutions. There was the Blue Coat School, founded in 1720 for the benefit of orphans, a School for the Blind, founded in 1791, the first of its kind anywhere in the world, an Infirmary and a Dispensary supported by charity, a Poor House, and a Seamen's Hospital 'for the maintenance of decayed seamen, their widows and children, supported by six pence a month out of the wages of every seaman sailing out of the port'.

The loss of privateering and slaving as sources of income did not, of course, spell the end of Liverpool, as those with vested interests to protect had gloomily predicted. During the next hundred years mere comfortable affluence would be converted to immense wealth, the population would increase ten-fold to 800,000 and the small Georgian town would become the Second City of the greatest empire in history. General trade continued as before, but the real upsurge in Liverpool's fortunes stemmed from cotton and the proximity of the Lancashire spinning and weaving towns. Starting with eight bales landed from an American ship in 1784, the cotton trade expanded rapidly until by 1852 imports through the port had reached 365,000 tons; likewise, Liverpool's warehousing and brokerage facilities gave it a virtual monopoly of the business. This suffered severely during the years of the American Civil War but recovered quickly thereafter. Other areas of import traffic developed during the nineteenth century included rubber, palm oil for soap and margarine, and meat, both on the hoof and refrigerated. Simultaneously, the Industrial Revolution had made the United Kingdom the workshop of the world and manufactured goods ranging from locomotives to thimbles streamed through the port bound for every quarter of the globe. The transition from sail to steam on the longest routes was complicated at first by the inability of the cargoes to pay for the dead space occupied by the engines and coal bunkers, but once the technical problems had been solved Liverpool steamers were able to enter Far Eastern markets and return with a profit. This process also resulted in the building of progressively larger vessels with more powerful engines.

Nor did the acquisition of new business stop with the import and export of goods. Emigration from the Old World to Australia, New Zealand, Canada, southern Africa and above all to the United States, was in full flow and this generated not only a demand for shipping but also a whole new and sometimes unscrupulous industry dedicated to supplying and housing the emigrants before they sailed. Between 1830 and 1930 it is estimated that nine million emigrants left Liverpool for America alone. In the closing decades of the century the small emigrant ships and packet vessels gave way to large passenger liners in which at least the first class passengers travelled in palatial comfort, especially on the transatlantic routes, which were dominated by Liverpool shipping lines.

Some of the men who created this wealth belonged to

local families who had made money during the previous century, but others had recognized Liverpool's potential and moved there in their youth. Often, their only assets on arrival were an education, a love of business for its own sake, and a total dedication to profit. Undoubtedly, they displayed complete ruthlessness as they clawed their way to the top of the mercantile ladder. They spent much time out of Liverpool in their chosen sphere of interest, be it the United States, South America, West Africa or the Far East, establishing lucrative trading conditions for their ships. Many became millionaires, some multi-millionaires; outside London, the only area which contained more millionaires than Liverpool was Clydeside. The author Nathaniel Hawthorne, who was the United States Consul in Liverpool from 1853 to 1857, met them both socially and professionally and commented that they were not gentlemen — at least according to the definitions of the day. They thought rather differently, set great store on their status and lived in some style. Certainly they considered themselves a cut above their Manchester neighbours, who were manufacturers; hence the old Lancashire saying, 'Liverpool Gentlemen and Manchester Men.' Be that as it may, they were firmly dedicated to the further development of the port so that it might yield yet more profit.

Canning Dock was completed in 1813, followed by Union Dock four years later, and then Prince's Dock, but it was not until the appointment of Jesse Hartley as the port's engineer that the system began to spread down-river towards the mouth of the estuary. Hartley enclosed the foreshore as far as the low-water mark, building immense cyclopean walls with granite blocks. Between 1832 and 1849 he added Brunswick, Waterloo, Victoria, Trafalgar, Albert, Canning Half-tide, Salisbury, Collingwood, Stanley, Nelson, Bramley Moore, Wellington, Sandon, Huskisson and Canada Docks to the system, increasing its water acreage from forty-six to 145. He then turned his attention to the Birkenhead and Wallasey dock systems, based on the ancient inlet which evolved into the East and West Floats, until a further

140 acres were available. In 1858 the administration of the Liverpool, Birkenhead and Wallasey dock estates, an undertaking already comparable to running a small city, was placed in the hands of the newly formed Mersey Docks and Harbour Board.

Continued expansion of trade and the increase in the size of ships meant that more docks had to be added to the north end of the Liverpool system; Canada Half-tide (renamed Brocklebank) in 1862, Langton and Alexandra in 1881 and Hornby in 1884. The southern docks, too, were modernized and added to, Herculaneum being opened in 1864, Harrington in 1883 and Toxteth in 1888. From the late 1840s onwards hydraulic power was progressively installed to work dock gates, movable bridges, cranes and warping capstans. The last, largest and most important element of the pre-World War II system, Gladstone Dock, was not opened until 1927. With the completion of this development the Dock Board's total water area amounted to 477 acres in Liverpool and 182 acres in Birkenhead, providing over thirty-eight miles of quays available to shipping, served by 121 miles of railway also owned by the Board, and backed by every kind of specialized handling and storage facility. Off the Pier Head, now the only place at which access to the river could be obtained from the town without passing through the docks, floated the Prince's Landing Stage, opened in 1856 and subsequently extended. This, connected to the land by covered gangways and a floating roadway, enabled some, but by no means all, ocean liners to berth alongside, whatever the state of the tide; the remainder, as an alternative to docking, anchored in mid-river, where they embarked and disembarked passengers, luggage and supplies by means of tenders. The Prince's Stage was also used by the steamers of the Isle of Man Steam Packet company, the Liverpool and North Wales Steamship Company, and by the numerous Mersey ferries carrying both passengers and vehicles.

Nor did the Mersey traffic end at Liverpool and Birkenhead. Throughout the nineteenth century Liverpool had exerted what amounted to a stranglehold on Manchester's overseas trade. Naturally, the latter resented the fact and in 1894 had responded with the Manchester Ship Canal, which diverged from the Mersey proper at Eastham Locks and ended in a dock complex in Manchester itself. In its passage the canal also served small dock systems at Ellesmere Port, Stanlow, and Runcorn. On the Wirral shore there were also small docks at Port Sunlight and nearby Bromborough, serving the Lever Brothers' soap, margarine and cattle-cake works. Upstream from Liverpool and on the Lancashire side was the port of Garston, exporting large quantities of coal and importing bananas, and Widnes docks, which dealt in coal, glass and chemicals.

Of course there was no point in developing dock and harbour facilities on this scale if they were not supported by an equally excellent inland transport infrastructure. Road transport played almost no part in the development of the port until recent times. So bad were the roads until the middle of the eighteenth century that anyone wishing to reach London was obliged to provide his own transport to Warrington and catch the stagecoach there; given a fair run, he might expect to reach the capital three days later. In the 1790s conditions had improved to the point that stages ran directly from Liverpool and reached London in two days, and in the 1830s the best coaches completed the journey in twenty-four hours. As mentioned earlier, the bulk transport of goods by road was almost impossible. Canals eased the situation, but they were slow and, as a result of the Industrial Revolution, the demand of the factories for raw materials was voracious. The need to increase the pace of commerce had become critical and, fortunately, technology also provided the means of satisfying that need.

The Liverpool and Manchester Railway, designed to expedite the transit of cotton and other goods between the two cities, was opened in 1830, the first railway in the world to connect two major centres of population and also the first to carry passengers as part of its daily routine. Such was its success that the whole country was soon in the grip of railway mania, resulting in the rapid construction of a rail network which reached into every corner of the kingdom, owned by private companies which competed fiercely with each other for business. In Liverpool the London and North Western Railway, the Lancashire and Yorkshire Railway and the Cheshire Lines Committee all established goods yards in close proximity to the docks, while on the Wirral joint lines operated by the LNWR and the Great Western Railway did likewise, with the Great Central Railway obtaining access at Seacombe. The largest of these companies, the LNWR, also laid out the huge marshalling yard at Edge Hill between 1875 and 1882. In this, incoming trains were broken up and their wagons and vans sent down to the docks, while traffic from the docks was assembled into outgoing trains, using gravity to assist in the shunting. Most of this work took place at night, with as many as sixty trains leaving for various destinations from Edge Hill alone.

As far as passenger traffic was concerned, the city was served by three major termini: the LNWR's Lime Street, the L&YR's Exchange and the CLC's Central. Riverside Station, adjacent to the Prince's Landing Stage and opened in 1895, was also operated by the LNWR over a tortuous route from Edge Hill, enabling passengers from the London boat trains to transfer to their steamers simply by crossing the platform to the gangway. Birkenhead was served by Woodside Station, situated close to the ferry stage. In addition to catering for long-distance travel, the railways also generated business for themselves by constructing comparatively minor lines along which suburban development took place; typical of these were the L&YR's lines from Liverpool to Ormskirk and Southport, and the Wirral Railway's lines from Birkenhead to New Brighton and West Kirby.

The accelerated pace at which commercial activity was being conducted led to a demand for faster communication between the two sides of the river than could be provided by the ferries. This resulted in the construction of the Mersey Railway, which was tunnelled from both ends in 1883/84, the tunnels meeting with only one inch difference between their centres. Opened by the Prince of Wales in 1886, the line was the world's first under-river railway and in 1903 became the first to convert from steam to electric traction. Originally running between James Street, Liverpool, and Hamilton Square, Birkenhead, the line was extended to Birkenhead Park in 1888 and to Liverpool Central in 1892, as well as putting out a branch to Rock Ferry.

Similar considerations led to the construction of the Liverpool Overhead Railway as a speedier means of travel along the dock system than the Dock Road, which was congested with horse-drawn vehicles of every kind. The first section of this, from Herculaneum to Alexandra Docks, was opened in 1893. The following year the line was extended northwards to Seaforth Sands and in 1896 the southern terminus was opened at Dingle. For some of its length, notably at the Pier Head, the line ran above the tracks of the Dock Board's lateral goods railway. The LOR employed electric traction from the outset and proved to be a great success, providing not only rapid transit for the thousands who had business in the docks, but also a tourist attraction which enabled visitors to see ships of every type from every maritime nation in the world loading and unloading their cargoes. For obvious reasons, the LOR was known as "The Dockers' Umbrella".

Concurrently, Merseyside was also developing its own domestic transport systems. In 1860 Birkenhead became the first town in the country to have its own street tramway. Trams began operating in Liverpool nine years later but Wallasey did not follow suit until 1879. Electrification commenced shortly before the turn of the century. The Liverpool tramway system was by far the largest and in 1911 owned 570 cars operating over 116 miles of track reaching into the outer suburbs; by way of contrast Birkenhead, its nearest rival, owned only sixty cars and 24 miles of track. In the 1930s the rapidly increasing number of motor vehicles on the streets began to cause congestion and both Wallasey and Birkenhead abandoned their trams in favour of more flexible motor buses. Liverpool had also introduced buses on certain routes but it declined to dismantle its tramway system, partly because it was profitable and partly because its replacement with buses would actually increase the number of public vehicles engaged in transportation and therefore add to the congestion. This decision was to result in a number of unexpected benefits during World War II.

The Mersey ferries were operated by the Birkenhead and Wallasey Corporations, the former running services from Woodside, Rock Ferry and New Ferry and the latter from Seacombe, Egremont and New Brighton. Even after the Mersey Railway had begun operating, many people preferred to travel by the ferries, which offered a pleasanter, healthier and certainly more interesting journey. During their busiest years the ferries carried over thirty million passengers per annum. In addition to their passenger services, the Corporations ran vehicle ferries from Seacombe and Woodside to the Prince's Stage. In 1901 350,000 vehicles were shipped across the Mersey in this way; by the early 1930s the figure had risen dramatically to 1,500,000 and, despite the introduction of new vessels, the service was in real danger of being swamped. It was this situation which had led to the construction of the first Mersey road tunnel, opened by King George V in 1934. There was, however, still plenty of traffic for the vehicle ferries to handle, as a large proportion of local heavy haulage was still made with horse-drawn wagons which could not, of course, make use of the tunnel. Again, the retention of the vehicle ferries, sometimes referred to as luggage boats because of their former use as tenders, was to provide a bonus during the war years.

It has sometimes been said that Liverpool reached the pinnacle of its affluence and power in 1914, but a closer examination reveals that no such pinnacle existed. There was, of course, constant change, but it tended to be social and demographic rather than financial. The city had long since flowed over the ridge and well beyond and it was no longer home to many of the entrepreneurial families which had amassed their wealth in Victoria's long reign. The most successful had left their Georgian terraces and purchased miniature country estates around the outskirts of the city and on the Wirral. Others, who were merely rich, moved to substantial mansions on Mossley Hill or around the edges of fashionable Princes and Sefton Parks. However, the pattern of business was changing. Hitherto, it had been conducted by the traditional Liverpool means of partnerships or syndicates, with members' shares expressed in sixty-fourths of the whole. Once undertakings became so vast that the demand for investment capital could no longer be met locally, it was inevitable that joint stock companies would be formed. These, ably managed by professional boards of directors on behalf of their shareholders, removed the need for the old families to reside locally. Some remained, retaining a personal interest in the running of the companies, but by the end of World War I it was clear that many were leaving. Liverpool was the poorer for their going, for the majority of the merchant princes were civic-minded in the extreme and throughout the nineteenth century had endowed hospitals, schools, libraries, art galleries and charitable institutions of every kind, both by subscription and bequest.

At the other end of the social spectrum were the seamen, dock workers and manual labourers, crammed into those parts of the old town which were not occupied by business premises, covering an area of approximately one and a half miles around the Pier Head and along the docklands to the north and south. Here there was often grinding poverty, deprivation and disease, aggravated by a system of casual labour. Seamen were discharged at the end of a voyage and might be re-employed or not, depending on circumstances. Dockers were even worse off, being picked for and paid for by the job, which might last only a few hours. It was a system which was wide open to petty corruption, nepotism and discrimination on religious or other grounds. In hard times, it was the women who kept the family afloat by working as chars, taking in washing or lodgers, or selling home-made produce. Underlying all was an intense distrust between Catholic and Protestant districts, stemming from the Hungry Forties when thousands of Irishmen had left their starving homeland in the hope of finding work in Liverpool. Other immigrant groups included Krumen, West African seamen who settled in Toxteth, close to the southern docks, and a small but growing Chinese community which established itself between them and the city centre. There was also a large Welsh population, attracted by the city's business opportunities, and this quickly made its mark in the building industry. Jewish immigrants, fleeing pogroms in eastern Europe and Russia at the turn of the century, recognized that Liverpool offered as much as the New World if one wanted a new start in life, and were soon assimilated into the city's commercial and professional life.

Comparatively few Welsh or Jewish arrivals settled in the inner areas, between which and the leafy domains of the rich lay a much broader belt of respectable terrace houses. In these lived the majority of the population, the skilled workers, the vast clerical staff required to administer the city's business, and indeed everyone in receipt of a regular income. In general, the more successful a man was in his career, the further from the city centre he resided.

Most Liverpool families had some connection with the sea, either by way of direct involvement or business. Everyone, without exception, understood that the city's living came from the sea. In addition to ships' officers and seamen, there were self-employed pilots, ship owners, ship builders, ship repairers, ship brokers, ships' chandlers and ships'victuallers; there were salvage experts, tug crews, dredger crews, lightermen, dockers, stevedores, dock gatemen and crane drivers; there were commodity brokers, freight agents, insurers, loss adjusters, bankers, solicitors, barristers, accountants, wine merchants, uniform tailors, office managers and clerks by the thousand; there were laundry workers, furnishers, upholsterers and decorators who serviced the passenger liners; and there was an army of warehousemen, carters and railwaymen to handle the goods that poured through the port in both directions. These goods included every raw material and artefact known to man; the dockers' joke about being asked to unload a scow with a cargo of dolls' eyes fell just short of reality. There was not a penny in the Sunday collection plate that had not been earned, directly or indirectly, from the sea.

Liverpool was a dynamic, bustling city with a raw masculine edge, and Jack Ashore was king for a day. He would arrive home with presents for all and a pocketful of money with which he would buy drinks for everyone in sight. The stories he told were of strange foreign ports, of bar-room brawls from which he emerged victorious, of sexual conquests in which his demanding partners all seemed to be fair and fortyish, and of cutting down the boatswain or the bucko mate with a few well-chosen words. Then, penniless, he would go back to sea. If Liverpool was not his home port, Jack was in some danger of being stripped of his wealth by crimps, pimps and likely lads. To protect him, the Sailors' Home was built in Canning Place; the prompt response of the disreputable element was to turn the surrounding area into a red light district. Among the most avid readers of the locally published and nationally respected Journal of Commerce were the city's whores, who wanted to know when and where the best paid ships were docking. Trouble could be had for the asking, but was contained by a police force which was notable as much for the physical size of its constables as for their understanding and ability to control the most difficult situations.

Above all, Liverpool was a city of contrasts. Those with great wealth walked the same pavements as those who had nothing. An almost puritanical respectability lived cheek by jowl with roaring vice. Even the Church of England, while still some years away from its graceless modern liturgy, nonetheless maintained an intentionally low-church stance to distance itself from the Roman Catholic High Mass. Again, commercial success was accompanied by an unequalled degree of social awareness, particularly in the fields of medicine and public health, enabling the city to claim a startling number of world and national firsts in these and related areas. These included the world's first school for the deaf and dumb (1825), the first society for the prevention of cruelty to animals (1841), the first slum-clearance scheme (1864), the first municipal housing (1869), and the first school of tropical medicine (1898). United Kingdom firsts included municipal baths (1829), the first medical officer of health (1847), the first street-cleaning department (1848), the first district nurse (1859), the first society for the prevention of cruelty to children (1883), the first home for epileptics (1889), the first public bacteriologist (1898), and the first anti-tuberculosis campaign (1901). The city's collective achievements in every field were a matter of intense pride to its citizens, yet this was expressed with a becoming modesty on the municipal crest: a Liver Bird on a shield with Neptune and a triton as supporters, accompanied by the motto *Deus Nobis Haec Otia Fecit*– God Made These Blessings For Us.

In terms of trade, World War I had two immediate effects. First, of the three million tons of British shipping lost as a result of enemy action, over half belonged to Liverpool. Secondly, foreign merchant fleets expanded by seven million tons, reducing the competitive edge of British shipping, and the business lost proved difficult to recover. There were, too, periods during the war when the dock system was so congested with vessels and cargoes that it almost ground to a standstill because so many skilled dock workers had enlisted in the armed services. It was not fully understood at the time that their best contribution to the national effort lay in the docklands rather than at the front, and the mistake was not allowed to happen a second time.

The Liverpool of 1939 was essentially the same city it had been in 1914. It had expanded its boundaries and large numbers of pleasant semi-detached villas, each with their own front and rear gardens, had been built in Allerton, Childwall, Crosby, Maghull, the Wirral and elsewhere, selling at £300 - £400 each and requiring only a small deposit to obtain possession. Further slum clearance had taken place and council housing estates were springing up around the city's outskirts. The effect was to reduce the population in the central areas, but in other respects little had changed. The port had weathered the worst effects of the Great War and the Depression and was once again on course, as was evidenced by the shipping statistics for the two years. In 1914, 24,756 vessels had entered the port, producing dues for the Dock Board of approximately £1,700,000; in 1939 the figures were 18,378 vessels and dues amounting to £2,583,460. However, the net registered tonnage for 1914 was 19,086,672 while that for 1939 was 21,724,050. Thus, any claim that the port was already in decline was premature; the ships were certainly fewer, but they were larger, faster and carried more. That Liverpool was still an excellent place for a man with vision was evidenced by the success of the Meccano company of Binns Road, manufacturing model engineering construction kits of the same name, Dinky die-cast model cars and Hornby model trains, all of which became instantly popular around the world.

This, then, was the Second City of Empire on the eve of the greatest and most terrible ordeal in its history.

2

Squaring Up

September 1939 - June 1940

The survival of Liverpool, and indeed every city and town in the land, depended upon the foresight, planning and administrative skills of its senior public servants. The Home Office had begun issuing circulars relating to Civil Defence as early as 1934 and since then Town Clerks had set about co-ordinating their resources and raising what amounted to local armies dedicated to preserving life and minimizing the effects of enemy air attack. From the end of 1937 onwards thousands of volunteers, from every walk of life, enrolled in one or other of the emergency services on a full- or part-time basis.

In each city and town the operational direction of Civil Defence services was the responsibility of a Controller who in turn reported to the Government's Regional Commissioner. In Liverpool, Birkenhead and Bootle it was the Town Clerk who served as Controller; in Litherland, Waterloo and Crosby it was the Clerk to the Lancashire County Council; in Wallasey it was the Chief Constable and in Bebington the Chief Constable of Cheshire. However, as the whole area was an entity in itself and capable of providing mutual support, the Town Clerk of Liverpool was also appointed Group Controller and was assisted by an Emergency Committee which included representatives from all the Civil Defence and technical services, including the gas, electricity, water and telephone authorities. Each Controller established a command and control post just outside what was imagined would be the immediate target area, and here reports would be received, resources applied as the situation demanded, and reinforcements requested from higher levels if they were needed.

In Liverpool, during normal times, the responsibility for the regular emergency services, including the Police, the Fire Brigade and the ambulance service, rested with the Watch Committee. The strength of the Liverpool City Police in December 1939 amounted to only 2,232 officers and men, which might be considered remarkably low, given the size and nature of the city; in fact, the strength of the force reached its wartime peak of 2,622 in December 1941 and four years later had fallen to 2,165. These were assisted by Special Constables who performed four hours' duty on the streets twice weekly; in September 1939 there were 1,360 Special Constables available, and for most of the war the numbers hovered around 700 and 800. At this period policing was still considered unsuitable work for a woman but in 1939 a Women's Auxiliary Police Corps was formed. This proved so useful that its initial strength of eighteen was raised to twenty-five in February 1942 and to ninety four months later. In addition to their normal duties of maintaining law and order and controlling the city's traffic, the police were required to take immediate local control of bombing incidents as they occurred, report the event to the Control Centre, co-ordinate emergency and rescue services, post guards to prevent the looting of damaged property, deal with survivors and inform next of kin of deaths or injuries. There was, in fact, no limit to the tasks they performed, nor to the initiative displayed by even the most junior ranks under fire.

The Liverpool Fire Brigade, another very remarkable force, was also to be in the forefront of the coming battle Prior to its formation as the Liverpool Police Fire Brigade in 1836, there were very limited municipal fire-fighting facilities and many of the town's fires were put out by the insurance companies' own firemen, who might or might not be interested if one's property was not insured with them. The insurance companies assisted in the foundation of the Brigade and contributed to its annual upkeep until 1941. Police ranks were used within the Brigade, whose members were universally known as Fire Bobbies. Yet, for all its emphasis on tradition, including burnished silver helmets for full-dress parades, the force was internationally respected for its pioneering techniques in fire fighting, equipment and operational drills, many of which were adopted by other brigades. The Brigade's primary task being the saving of life, all its planning was devoted to ensuring a rapid response and the availability of water resources at the site of the fire. One feature, unique to Liverpool at the time, was the role of the gateman who, once a call had been received, would start the engine of the responding appliance even before the crew had reached it, then halt the traffic outside the station. Another, equally unique, was the waterman, an employee of the water authority who either travelled with the appliance to the fire or lived close to the responding station and was able to advise on the current state of local mains, hydrants and pressures. Again, when salt-water swimming baths were built by the Corporation prior to World War I the Brigade had insisted that double hydrants be positioned at regular intervals along the main connecting the baths with the pumping station at the Pier Head, and this was to yield immense benefits when the enemy attacks began. Further benefits were inadvertently provided by the IRA's terrorist gangs when they started a campaign of arson within the city in 1921, since this led to the Merseyside Fire Brigades' Mutual Aid Scheme, ensuring the prompt support of brigades as far distant as Warrington and Preston; this model served as the basis for the much larger Fire Brigades' Regional Reinforcement Scheme developed during World War II.

In 1939 the Brigade consisted of 255 officers and men manning stations at Hatton Garden, which also housed the Brigade Headquarters and Control Room, Westminster Road, Durning Road, Derby Lane, Essex Street,

Longmoor Lane, Banks Road, All Saints Road, Orphan Drive and Mather Avenue, the last housing a duplicate Control Room which could be activated in an emergency. Communication between the Control Room and outlying units was maintained by telephone, despatch rider and runner. In the Control Room itself the Mobilizing Officer kept a careful watch on the deployment of the Brigade's assets and once a pre-determined level had been reached would call forward neighbouring brigades to assist, their units being met at the city boundary by despatch riders who would lead them to the area in which they were needed.

The Brigade was also responsible for training many hundreds of men belonging to the part-time Auxiliary Fire Service in straightforward fire-fighting techniques. The AFS Headquarters was located in Pioneer Building, Dale Street, and by 1940 there were over fifty AFS stations, with up to three appliances each, located in every district in the city. Most were in school premises with the appliances kept under shelters in the playground, but others used commercial garages and some, like those at the Pier Head, Rose Lane, Coburg, Canada, Huskisson and Prince's Docks, were purpose built.

Working closely with the Brigade and with a neighbouring headquarters in Hatton Garden was the Liverpool Salvage Corps, formed in 1842 and also funded by insurance companies. The Salvage Corps specialized in recovering goods and minimizing loss at commercial premises damaged by fire and other perils, and its ranks contained many qualified tradesmen. In 1939 the Corps volunteered en bloc for service with the AFS but its work was considered to be so important that the following year it reverted to its original role.

Prior to the outbreak of war three types of ambulance operated in the city: the emergency ambulance service, controlled by the Watch Committee, the Penny-in-the-Pound ambulances, which provided transport to and from hospital for subscribers, and the green "fever" ambulances which carried isolation cases. The service was rationalized and expanded to meet the anticipated need, the shortfall in drivers being met by women volunteers who had at least some experience of driving the family car.

Ambulances were despatched to incidents in which there were known to be casualties. At the incident they would be met by the first line of medical defence, the first aid parties. These were deployed as required by the Control Centre and consisted of four men and a driver, all of whom were volunteers who had been trained in first aid techniques, including members of the Red Cross and St John's Ambulance Service. Having given such assistance as they could, the first aid parties were at first required to decide which casualties could be released and which should be transported by the ambulances to the nearest first aid post or to hospital, depending on the severity of the case. Later, this responsibility was assumed by an "incident doctor" despatched to the scene.

The first aid posts were set up throughout the city on the approximate basis of one for every 15,000 inhabitants. They were manned by doctors, nurses and nursing auxiliaries who completed the diagnoses and immediate treatment. In direct reserve were mobile first aid units which might be despatched to a particularly bad incident or to reinforce a post in danger of being swamped by casualties. Finally, there were the hospitals themselves, supplemented by recently established emergency hospitals, organized permanently to cope with a sudden flow of critically injured.

Rescue squads were also formed for despatch to incidents as the situation demanded. The volunteers joining these came from the building and civil engineering industries, partly because of the heavy nature of the work, and partly because the risks involved in tunnelling through the wreckage of a building required careful technical assessment. These included not only the danger of further collapse, but of electrocution by exposed cables and asphyxiation by escaping gas; sometimes, the rubble itself might still be smouldering. Every step towards those trapped below required a decision upon which life depended. On many occasions, the reward would be lives saved, but on others the final breakthrough would reveal only horror. Yet, even when the carnage was at its worst, there would never be a shortage of men willing to undertake such work.

The largest group of Civil Defence volunteers were, of course, the Air Raid Precautions (ARP) Wardens. In September 1939 Liverpool possessed 2,560 full-time, paid wardens and 15,740 part-time volunteer wardens. At the head of the service was the Chief Warden, responsible directly to the city's Chief Constable. Below him were the Divisional Wardens, each responsible for an area which, following standard Civil Defence procedure, was based on the boundaries of a police division. The divisions were sub-divided into a total of forty-one groups, each led by a Group Warden, and these were further sub-divided into 748 sectors. Each sector contained a permanently manned sector post, some of which were purpose-built, although the majority were located in existing buildings and reinforced with sandbag walls. The principal task of the warden was to act as the eyes and ears of the Control Centre, reporting the extent and nature of damage within his sector, as well as assessing the local need for assistance by the emergency and rescue services. In addition, he was responsible for enforcing the blackout regulations, maintaining a watch on the public air raid shelters and assisting the police to evacuate property in the area of unexploded bombs. After the raid he was responsible for directing those who had been rendered homeless to the nearest relief centre. As he often lived within his sector his intimate knowledge of the area and its people was invaluable. Often, only he knew where to find the occupants of bomb-damaged property, and it was to him that people came when searching for missing relatives and friends. As the war continued the wardens were also required to form street fire-fighting parties and train them in the correct use of the stirrup pump and sand bucket. By the time the Luftwaffe's attacks had reached their peak over 53,000 people had been formed into 6,226 such parties, and thanks to their efforts many potentially disastrous fires were extinguished before they took hold. A further 50,000 people were trained in fire-watching duties, which they undertook nightly by rota at their place of work.

Many people appreciated that in the event of a major enemy air attack the telephone system, upon which the Civil Defence services relied heavily, would be so seriously disrupted that runners would become the only reliable means of communication. With this in mind, Professor H.J. Channon of Liverpool University formed the Liverpool Civil Defence Cadet Corps from teenage boys who volunteered for the task on a part-time basis. By October 1940 some 2,000 boys had been trained not only in the accurate delivery of messages, but also in fire fighting, anti-gas drill and first aid. Initially, the corps relied on about 250 privately owned bicycles, but was later joined by 100 motor-cyclists. In due course it evolved into the Civil Defence Messenger Service and, when the telephone system was destroyed in May 1941, its members performed their vitally important task willingly and efficiently, more often than not under fire.

Together, the Police, Fire Brigade, Ambulance Service, First Aid teams, Rescue parties, Warden Service and Messengers provided the first echelon of Civil Defence. The second echelon consisted of those services responsible for people whose homes had been destroyed by enemy action. Rest Centres, staffed by the Women's Voluntary Service and equipped with mattresses and blankets, were set up in church halls around the city by Mr G.W. Molyneux, the Chief Public Assistance Officer, and to these the victims would be brought by the police and wardens. Most would be in a state of shock and were given tea and allowed to rest, then provided with a cooked meal. Many had lost everything they owned save the clothes they stood up in, and since these were often no longer fit for further use they were replaced from depots set up by the Public Assistance Committee, stocked with clothing supplied by the British War Relief Society and donors overseas. Finally, they were given a small sum of money to meet their immediate needs and became the responsibility of the Billeting Service.

This was established by the city's Chief Building Officer, Mr George Binns, with the assistance of volunteers and his team of sanitary inspectors who, during the period between the outbreak of war and the start of the German air attacks, carried out an immense house-to-house survey and listed every available billet. Billeting Officers would visit the Rest Centres on the morning after a raid and direct the homeless towards their next lodging. This, however, was simply a temporary measure, since rehousing was the final objective. To this end, empty Corporation houses were reserved for the victims of bomb damage and untenanted private houses were also requisitioned. Once the refugees had moved in, the Corporation would supply them with sufficient essential furniture to make a new start. Tragically, there were families who would be bombed out of their homes not once or twice, but three and more times. Again, while the Billeting Service was a by-word for efficiency, when the enemy mounted his main attack it was so severely strained that almost 10,000 people had to be found accommodation in neighbouring towns which were not under such intense pressure.

Last, but by no means least, there were the drivers of the mobile canteens, many of which were gifts from the Dominions or the United States. They served tea, sandwiches and even scouse, and their arrival at an incident site after a difficult and dangerous journey over the rubble was more than welcomed by the utterly exhausted fire fighters and rescue squads.

The provision of air raid shelters, both private and public, had begun even before the war started. In 1939 Liverpool could accommodate 180,650 people in domestic shelters and a further 33,750 in public shelters; these figures continued to rise steadily until in May 1944 they reached their respective peaks of 700,510 and 80,204. Domestic shelters were of two types. The Anderson shelter was made from corrugated iron and erected over a specially dug trench in a back garden, the spoil being used to provide head cover; the trench was deep enough to accommodate bunks but, unless it was lined with concrete, it would quickly become damp and unhealthy; ideally, its entrance would be fronted by a sandbag wall The Morrison shelter was designed for easy erection within the house and consisted of a steel plate, girder and mesh cube capable of supporting the collapsed building until a rescue squad arrived. Public shelters were normally situated in the basements of substantial buildings, generally in the city centre, but others were purpose-built with brick walls and concrete slab roofs in parks and side streets; in either case, an essential feature was the provision of escape manholes. Most shelters were proof against blast and comparatively near misses, but only the deepest offered a defence against a direct hit. Curiously, neither of the Mersey Railway's underground stations in Liverpool, James Street and Central, were taken into service as shelters until after the air raids had started. On 12 October 1940 the *Liverpool Daily Post* proudly announced that the city was leading the country in the provison of steel bunks and wire mattresses for its public shelters. Thus far, six shelters had been so equipped, and a further 10,000 steel bunks were on their way, plus 30,000 wooden bunks.

Many people preferred the public shelters because of the camaraderie engendered by shared danger and hardship, and some of the street shelters were fitted out very comfortably by their regular users. During periods of prolonged air attack families would go to the shelter at dusk and be joined there by their breadwinner on his return from work. At first sanitation was a problem in the larger public shelters but the Emergency Committee set up a Shelter Welfare Service under the Public Health Department and the appropriate facilities, plus hot and cold water and cooking stoves, were provided. Bedding left on bunks instead of being taken home during the day soon became verminous and this practice also required regulating. Overcrowding, too, was an early problem Incredible as it may seem today, many people travelled from the relative safety of the suburbs, and even from the Wirral, to obtain a place in a public shelter in the infinitely more dangerous city centre, simply because of a perverse and totally unfounded belief that it offered greater protection. Once shelter registers had been compiled many such individuals were found to have either domestic shelters of their own or access to adequate public shelters in their neighbourhood; they were told to use these in future, a step which eased the crowding considerably. Shelter life had its own code of conduct, and its compensations too. There were parties, sing-songs, quizzes, games, radios and gramophones and, sometimes, great events like a birth.

One of the best air raid shelters I have ever seen lay in the grounds of my old school, Liverpool College. Not far from the chapel where, throughout the war, the names of old boys killed in action or decorated for gallantry were announced during the daily services, lay a small piece of woodland known as the Glade, which provided a suitable site. The architect of the shelter was the remarkable Harold Lickes, Vice-Master and Head of the Lower School. During World War I he had served on the Western Front with the King's Own Yorkshire Light Infantry and in 1939, knowing exactly what was required to obtain protection against the heaviest bombardment, he put the experience to good use. Having acquired a large quantity of railway sleepers and stout timber balks, he built a series of interconnected dug-out tunnels in the Glade, covering the whole structure with several feet of earth. The complex had four entrances, so that if one or more were destroyed by enemy action, the others would serve as escape routes. Within, the tunnels changed direction at right angles every few yards, confusing the uninitiated, but this was intended to contain the blast effect of a direct hit within a small area, and would undoubtedly have done so. Although the shelter never sustained such a hit, when a parachute mine blasted a huge crater only yards distant, it withstood the impact undamaged.

Civil Defence measures were also taken throughout the docks, where the wartime controlling body was the Port Emergency Committee. This had been established on the instructions of the Committee of Imperial Defence in August 1936, when the drift to war was already apparent, and its function then had been to examine the various problems which would arise in the event of hostilities with Germany. These included the probable diversion of traffic from the east coast ports to Liverpool, adjusting the port's normal working arrangements to fit the convoy system, and the difficulties likely to be encountered as a result of enemy air attack. The Committee received its executive powers from the Minister of War Transport on 23 August 1939, some days before the war actually commenced. Its primary task was to mobilize the assets of the port so as to ensure the quickest possible turn-round of vessels using the docks and the speedy clearance of their cargoes. As might be expected of a body responsible for facilities of critical national importance, its constitution reflected every aspect of the port's workings and included representatives of the Mersey Docks and Harbour Board, the shipping lines, both deep water and coastal, the port labour force, including management and unions, the railways, the canals, the Royal Navy's Flag Officer, the supply transport officer, the road haulage officer, the food movement officer and HM Customs. It had the power to allocate the labour force where it was needed most, to control warehouse space, and to eliminate sectional interests for the better running of the port. Later, the Minister of War Transport was to appoint a Regional Port Director as his personal representative, with wide-ranging powers which included the settling of priorities. As mentioned earlier, the system of casual labour within the docks generated both abuse and resentment, but from 1941 this grievance was removed when all registered dock workers became employees of the Ministry of War Transport, a step which resulted in greater efficiency. Such restrictive practices as remained were eliminated for the duration of the war by the Minister of Labour in the Churchill government, Mr Ernest Bevin. The critical labour shortage which had afflicted the port during World War I was avoided by placing dock workers on the Reserved Occupation Schedule, which prohibited their enlisting in the armed services, although many would willingly have done so. The Admiralty had introduced convoys on the outbreak of war but, while this served its purpose of containing shipping losses, it also disrupted the natural rhythm of the port's operations. Normally, perhaps a dozen ships would arrive at the Bar with each tide, and the same number would be undocked and head out to sea. After convoys had been introduced, however, only coastal traffic and a handful of independently routed ships would be handled for several tides in a row. Then, suddenly, a convoy of up to fifty ships would arrive, all of varying types and dimensions, for which the correct berths had to be found.

Simultaneously, occupied berths had to be cleared in readiness and vessels made ready for sea. This dual movement was further complicated first by the fact that the larger vessels, inward or outward bound, could only use the dock entrances during the two-and-a-half hours either side of high water, in other words for ten hours out of twenty-four, and secondly because high priority vessels had first call of the tugs. Yet, although there were times when the docks, the river and its approaches might appear to be hopelessly congested, the port continued to function efficiently in accordance with a carefully conceived procedure. A senior member of the Dock Board was permanently based at the Admiralty's Shipping Diversion Room in London, which maintained track of incoming convoys and decided upon their port of arrival. He maintained constant telephone contact with the Harbour Master's Department, and was thus able to provide several days' warning of arrivals, followed by classified memoranda containing full details of each vessel's cargo and its location within the holds. This information was discussed at the Harbour Master's daily conferences and the appropriate decisions were taken long before the convoy had reached the Bar. Additional burdens which were shouldered by the Harbour Master's Department included the provision of berths for the Royal Navy's minesweeping and escort vessels, and also on occasion for capital ships, aircraft carriers and cruisers, and the allocation of graving docks, where the competing claims of shipowners and the Navy had to be reconciled and accorded priority.

The purely military aspect of Merseyside's defences contained various elements, not all of which were apparent at the time, for obvious reasons. The approach channels to the port were covered by four 6-inch guns, two in Fort Perch Rock at New Brighton and two in a permanent emplacement on the Lancashire shore known as Fort Crosby. These weapons fired a 100-pound shell to a maximum accurate range of 6,000 yards, assisted by optical range-finders. Fort Perch Rock also contained four searchlights, each believed to be of six million candlepower. Two were movable lights. one being mounted on top of the East Tower and the other direclty below it; the remaining two were fixed beams built into the base of the original South Tower, illuminating the area across the river mouth to Gladstone Dock. An electrically activated minefield, controlled from ashore, was also laid between New Brighton and Gladstone Dock, and this was covered by torpedo tubes concealed on the New Brighton landing stage.

Defence against air attack involved all three services Most obvious was the balloon barrage, which had an ideal density of nine balloons per mile. This was the responsibility of the RAF, which established sites on any suitable open space within and around the city. These were generally manned by personnel of the Women's Auxiliary Air Force (WAAF). The standard low zone balloon was sixty-two feet long and twenty-five feet in diameter, holding 19,000 cubic feet of hydrogen. It was flown from a mobile winch to an altitude of 5,000 feet, the rate of ascent and descent being 400 feet per minute, and when not in action was kept close-hauled at 500 feet. It was appreciated that on their own the balloon and cable did not present a serious threat, even if struck directly by a modern aircraft, and to remedy this double parachutes were attached to the cable, which was fitted with separation links below the balloon and above the winch. Thus, when a cable was struck it would tear itself free and be towed along at a speed which would open the parachutes; the effect of the sudden application of negative forces could be compared to flying into a solid wall and the enemy aircraft would sustain fatal damage as a result. Balloons, however, were vulnerable to winds of over sixty miles per hour, which would cause them to break free and vanish over the horizon, and to strikes by lightning, which would instantly turn them into a tumbling fireball of blazing hydrogen.

Life on a balloon site could be unbearably dull, even when the site was close to the city. On one site, manned by WAAFs, one of the girls was about to be married and, it being a quiet evening with no prospect of enemy action, the rest decided to celebrate the event with her in the local pub. When they returned, jolly but much the worse for wear, they tumbled into bed. Next morning, a late reveille was enlivened by a sudden shriek of 'The balloon's gone!' The girls raced from their billet, but they were several hours too late and, in all probability, the wandering blimp was well on its way to Sweden; all that remained were several hundred feet of cable, mute but irrefutable evidence of their guilt. Their commanding officer was not amused, but he was restricted as to the form of punishment he could mete out to female personnel. His solution, however, fitted the crime exactly and was diabolical in its ingenuity. The entire site crew were posted to wild, remote, wind-blasted, cliff-top sites on the east coast of Scotland, as far removed from the fleshpots of Walton as he could send them!

An equally obvious defence against air attack were the anti-aircraft guns, manned by the Royal Artillerymen of General Sir Frederick Pile's Anti-Aircraft Command Specifically, Merseyside fell within the operational area of the 4th Anti-Aircraft Division, commanded by Major-General C.A.E. Cadell, whose responsibilities included the West Midlands and the North West.

The four types of anti-aircraft guns employed were the 3.7-inch, firing 28-pound shells at the maximum rate of ten per minute to an effective ceiling of 25,000 feet, with a lethal burst radius of fifteen yards; the 4.5-inch, firing 55-lb shells at the maximum rate of eight per minute to an effective ceiling of 26,000, with a lethal burst radius of twenty yards; the 3-inch, a reconditioned World War I naval weapon with an effective engagement ceiling of 14,000 feet; the forty-millimetre Bofors, firing two-lb impact-fused high-explosive shells at the rate of 120 per minute to a ceiling of 12,000 feet, above which they exploded automatically; and the Lewis machine gun, another World War I weapon, mounted singly or in pairs, for defence against low-level attack. Because of their tremendous muzzle blast, which would shatter windows and even cause structural damage, the heavy anti-aircraft guns were deployed around the outer edge of Liverpool and the Wirral towns, generally in groups of four, but sometimes on sites with two, six or eight guns The smaller 40mm Bofors guns were less anti-social neighbours and were generally sited in the public parks. Each gunsite was equipped with a range-finder and predictor, the latter containing an analogue computer which passed ballistic data to the guns. At night, sound locators were used in conjunction with searchlights. In 1939 the standard searchlight had a diameter of 96 centimetres and its carbon projector produced 210 million candlepower, but 150-centimetre searchlights with 510 million candlepower were later used in conjunction with radar.

The principal object of anti-aircraft fire was, of course, to destroy or damage hostile aircraft, but it also reduced the enemy's bombing accuracy by forcing him to attack from high altitude and take evasive action, as well as breaking up his formations so that the RAF's fighters could engage with greater effect. Nevertheless, it is important to remember that the anti-aircraft gunners were attempting to hit a distant, fast-moving target which was travelling in three dimensions, and generally under cover of darkness, at a period when radar and operational computers were still in their infancy. Thus, anti-aircraft gunnery was as yet far from being an exact science, and the results it produced were small in relation to the effort expended. On the other hand, it did produce results.

The area above the guns' effective ceiling was the responsibility of RAF Fighter Command's No. 12 (later No.9) Group. It was appreciated from the outset that Merseyside lay beyond the range at which the Luftwaffe's fighter squadrons could protect their bomber fleets and, that being the case, most German air activity over the area would take place at night, with the exception of daylight reconnaissance flights which might drop a few bombs for nuisance value. Airfields which provided local night-fighter defence included Speke, on the outskirts of Liverpool; Squires Gate, near Blackpool; Cranage, Cheshire; Tern Hill and High Ercall, Shropshire; Wrexham, Denbighshire; and Valley, Anglesey. The aircraft most commonly used were the Hawker Hurricane and the Boulton Paul Defiant, joined later by the Bristol Blenheim and the Bristol Beaufighter. The Hurricane, a high-performance, single-seater fighter with a maximum speed of 316 mph and an armament of eight wing-mounted machine guns, was not altogether suitable for the role and was replaced by the Defiant, which became the most numerous night fighter over the North West. The Defiant was a two-seater fighter with a maximum speed of 303 mph and its armament of four machine guns was housed in a power-operated turret immediately behind the cockpit The Blenheim was a twin-engined aircraft with a crew of three; it had a maximum speed of 260 mph and was armed with four machine guns in a fixed mounting beneath the fuselage. The Beaufighter, another twin-engined design with a three-man crew, was a much superior machine which entered service with the RAF in August 1940. It had a maximum speed of 333 mph and mounted four twenty-millimetre cannon in the nose plus six machine guns in the wings. Small numbers became available towards the end of the Luftwaffe's raids on Merseyside.

Airborne interception radar, which, when fitted to night fighters, enabled them to locate and destroy their opponents, had existed for some years, but its issue was as yet by no means general and, during the period of German air attacks on Liverpool, most radar-equipped units were deployed in the south and east of England This meant that the local night-fighter squadrons were forced to rely on a less efficient means of interception. Once the raiders had crossed the coast their progress was tracked by the Observer Corps, which reported to Fighter Command Group and Sector operations rooms. As the raiders approached a sector the night fighters would be scrambled and, using height and directional data supplied by ground radar, their controller would vector them towards the enemy. The problems were similar to those experienced by the anti-aircraft gunners in that the hunt took place in three dimensions, and in darkness, with a strong possibility that those involved would miss each other completely. In the final analysis, interception depended upon the keen eyes of the night-fighter crews. The majority of interceptions took place miles from Liverpool, while the raiders were on their way to or returning from the target, and the civilians knew little of them save for the following day's reports of enemy aircraft destroyed. There were occasions, however, when those in the shelters would hear the ear-splitting roar of one aircraft in low-level pursuit of another, accompanied by the hammering of multiple machine guns as a night fighter hounded his quarry to destruction, and, like the sound of the anti-aircraft guns in full voice, it was immensely reassuring.

Nevertheless, whatever the deterrent value of the defences, it was clear that most bombers would get through to their targets. Given this unpleasant fact, it would obviously be better if the enemy could be persuaded by decoys to unload his bombs uselessly while still incurring the risks and losses inherent in mounting a raid. This was the thinking which led to the widespread construction of decoy fire sites under the codename of Starfish. These were located in areas which bore some similarity to the target itself and consisted of re-usable building-shaped structures of steel and asbestos, covered with tarred roofing felt, plus drums containing other combustible material, including coal, paraffin and creosote. As soon as the target itself came under attack, orders would be telephoned from the Control Centre for the decoy fires to be lit. This was done electrically from a concrete pillbox about 600 yards from the decoy. If all went well, the enemy's pathfinder fires in the real target area would be extinguished quickly and the follow-up bomber squadrons would attack the decoy. Liverpool's Starfish site was located on the sands of the Dee estuary, close to the Wirral shore, and succeeded in attracting many bombs which would otherwise have landed in the city.

Bomb Disposal Squads were also formed by the Royal Engineers to deal with unexploded bombs, and by the Royal Navy to deal with unexploded mines, the latter having been dropped by parachute for use in the port's approaches but drifted inland during their fall. Many failed to explode because of malfunction, but some were fitted with delayed detonation timing devices with a view to sapping civilian morale, while others contained anti-handling devices and were specifically intended to kill the bomb disposal personnel. Those living in the area surrounding an unexploded bomb had to be evacuated to nearby Rest Centres until experts had rendered it safe, often in terribly dangerous circumstances.

Although the period between September 1939 and May 1940 is sometimes referred to as the Phoney War, at sea the contest was fought in deadly earnest from the outset. The destruction of the pocket-battleship *Admiral Graf Spee* in the aftermath of the Battle of the River Plate was certainly encouraging, as was the elimination of so much of the German surface fleet off Norway in April 1940, but the principal menace remained the U-boat and the pattern which was emerging gave grounds for the most serious concern. In simple terms, the construction of new British merchant vessels could not keep pace with the rate at which the existing stock was being sunk; simultaneously, construction of U-boats had begun to exceed losses by a wide margin. It was true that most of the merchant shipping loss fell on independently routed vessels, which were either too fast or too slow to be incorporated in escorted convoys, but the convoys themselves were being subjected to heavier attacks and the eventual outcome of the Battle of the Atlantic could not be predicted. Responsibility for providing protection for shipping in the eastern Atlantic rested with Admiral Sir Martin Dunbar-Nasmith, the Commander-in-Chief Western Approaches, whose headquarters were, for the moment, located in Plymouth. In Liverpool, the major Western Approaches port, the non-arrival of expected vessels and the sight of damaged ships limping home both confirmed the trend of the battle.

Yet, for the majority, the war remained something of a non-event, intruding on their lives only to the extent of the restrictions it imposed. Places of entertainment were soon allowed to reopen once it was clear that the people were behind the Government and there would be no danger of public unrest. The evacuees settled down to write their first letters home; some were to make lifelong friends of the families with whom they were billeted, some were cruelly exploited for the allowances they brought and, when it seemed that there was no danger after all, some simply came home. People got used to carrying identity cards, ration books and gasmasks, erected domestic shelters, put up blackout curtains and covered their windows with diamond-shaped patterns of sticky brown paper tape to minimize the danger from flying glass; close-mesh netting was glued to the windows of trams and buses for the same reason, leaving small peepholes for passengers to see where they were. The worst hazard was the blackout, in which all vehicles drove on masked headlights and without the benefit of street lighting. Despite the liberal use of white paint on kerbs, lamp posts, fenders and mudguards, fatal accidents were numerous. After dusk, pedestrians carried an electric torch, wore something white and relied heavily on their ears. In the docks, where the path of the unwary was strewn with dangers at the best of times, the chances of accidental death or injury were much higher. Most people got on with their jobs and volunteered for some aspect of Civil Defence or other war work in their spare time. There was, however, one unwelcome visitor whose appearance in a street would bring neighbours silently to their doors, and he was the telegraph boy on his bicycle; all too often, his little orange envelope would contain an official statement of regret informing next of kin that a serviceman had been killed, wounded or was missing on active service.

Phoney War or not, Liverpool was the scene of a great deal of clandestine activity which was of national importance, and much of it was centred on the area of Edge Lane. Here, the extensive premises of Littlewoods Pools were commandered on the outbreak of war for use by MC5, the postal censorship service, which examined correspondence to and from neutral countries, including mail intended for Germany. The specially selected staff included experts in every known language, cryptanalysts and specialists in a wide variety of fields. Altogether, about 2,000 people were employed by MC5, including many recruited locally, the qualities sought being intelligence and the ability to detect information which might be of use to the enemy, and irregularities which indicated the use of concealed codes. Some 100,000 letters were examined daily at Edge Lane, while at Aintree parcels and packages containing books and periodicals were similarly scrutinized in the premises of Vernons Pools. Each day, approximately 100 letters attracted the suspicion of the examiners, who would pass them on to their supervisors. They, in turn, would pass them on to the linguists and cryptanalysts, who possessed constantly updated lists of every known code, or to the laboratory, which was equipped to detect invisible inks of every type.

Some of the means by which agents attempted to communicate information were ingenious in the extreme. One used postal chess games to encode his messages, but was exposed by the illogical moves; another sent flower drawings with messages encoded in the details of the foliage, but was foiled by an examiner with botanical

1. A pre-war aerial photograph of the world-famous waterfront showing: the Liver building (A/B); the Cunard building (C); the Mersey Docks and Harbour Board building (D); the floating roadway to the landing stage (F); the circles of the tram terminus (G, H, J).

2. Another view of the waterfront illustrating the great length of the landing stage. To the left of the Liver building is the spire of St Nicholas' parish church, while to the right the unfinished bulk of the Cathedral towers over the city. The white ferry is *Royal Daffodil II* in her river cruise livery.

3. Inspection pits, roofed with timber balks, provided ready-made shelters for workers at tramway depots. For additional protection a tramcar could be driven over the top. The shelter's equipment is completed by wooden benches and roll-down anti-gas curtains.

4. A Convoy Conference at HQ Western Approaches, located beneath Derby House. The masters of merchant vessels due to sail receive their briefing from Royal Navy Officers.

5. The nation's lifeline. During the war, the port handled no less than 1,285 inwards-bound convoys, consisting of ships of every description.

6. The wreckage of James Street Station on the Overhead Railway after an enemy attack.

7. Recovery of a fire engine from a bomb crater in Roe Street. The crew were killed in this incident.

8. Rubble blocking the streets of the principal shopping area to a depth of several feet. The building is the gutted skeleton of Blackler's store.

9. Cook Street in the heart of the city's commercial quarter, with the Bank of England on the left. On the right are the remains of the Cook Street Arcade, the basement of which was cleared of rubble and turned into an Emergency Water Supply cistern resembling a Roman Bath.

10. The calcined wreckage of Lewis's store after the worst of the debris had been cleared and the building made safe. Access to two of the flagpoles on the roof was possible and the management defiantly flew the Union Jack from these.

11. *Silver Sandal* on fire in the river with fire-boat standing by.

12. The fire aboard *Silver Sandal* showing the vessel's deck cargo of fighter aircraft..

13. The salvage vessel *Salvor* assists in raising *Royal Daffodil II* at Seacombe Landing Stage. Note the barrage balloon in the distance.

14. *Liscard,* one of several old vehicle ferries ingeniously equipped to handle deck cargoes of aircraft by the addition of a derrick.

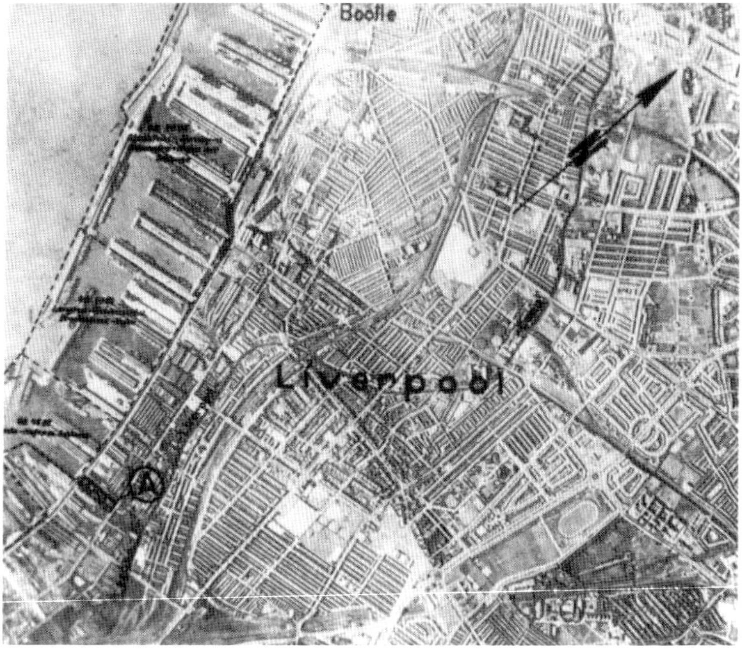

15. German air-reconnaisance photograph showing the northern end of the Liverpool dock system. Bomb damage is clearly indicated by the pale irregular patches.

16. A busy scene at Gladstone Dock during the latter half of the war. The berthed ships include liners, cargo vessels, an aircraft-carrier and a cruiser. The area in the foreground, occupied by private houses and timber yards until devastated by the blitz, has been cleared and now contains storage sheds.

knowledge; another, gramophone records in which the singer inserted a few lines of his own; others used embroidered garments to convey information with a special pattern of stitches, but this was soon picked up by needlework experts; others, again, wrote harmless letters but concealed their information beneath the stamps, tearing the perforations in a certain way to indicate they had done so, only to have their efforts exposed by ultra-violet rays. MC5 continued to function throughout the war and was responsible for the detention of numerous agents and Nazi sympathizers. Some were permitted to remain at liberty for a while, their correspondence with German intelligence post boxes in neutral countries being carefully doctored to provide a flow of misinformation. The full extent of the department's wartime activities has never been disclosed.

Also off Edge Lane was the factory of the Automatic Telephone and Electric Company where, in conditions of great secrecy, a distant reading gyro-magnetic compass was being developed for the RAF, to be used in conjunction with a bomb-sight and auto-pilot produced by the Royal Aircraft Establishment at Farnborough. From the outset, testing the sensitive components proved impossible because of the magnetic fields set up by the factory's own electrical equipment, and when the scientists attempted to continue their tests in the open they were equally frustrated by further electrical fields generated by the overhead wires of the neighbouring tram depot. It was decided, therefore, to establish a laboratory in a house at 51 Freehold Street, off Prescot Road, which lay beyond the magnetic influence of the factory or the tramways. The question of security was paramount and, rather than risk drawing attention to the project with elaborate precautions, a very low-key approach was adopted. Daily, the part for testing was concealed in a bundle of clean laundry and wheeled in a pram by an unsuspecting cleaner from the factory to the laboratory. For the return journey, the cleaner collected a bundle of dirty laundry which contained a tested part.

It was very simple and, if either the cleaners or their friends chose to examine the “baby”, the component on its own told them nothing. Freehold Street was seriously damaged by air attack in November 1940, but No. 51 survived. The compass proved to be a great success, being used on the Dams Raid and in the Battle of the Atlantic, and was also taken into service by the US Army Air Force.

On 10 May 1940 the Phoney War ended when the Wehrmacht invaded France and the Low Countries. Its offensive was brilliantly conceived, turning the Allied deployment to its own advantage, and was boldly executed. In a matter of days a concentrated drive by the German armour had reached the Channel coast, cutting the Allied armies in two. The small Dutch Army, fighting in isolation, surrendered on 14 May. When the Belgian Army followed suit on 27 May the British Expeditionary Force and the French armies in Belgium were effectively trapped in a shrinking pocket centred on Dunkirk.

In London, Neville Chamberlain resigned on 10 May and was replaced by Winston Churchill. The stark reality of the situation was explained to the Cabinet by its military advisors and, suddenly, the consequences of the years when politicans had deliberately neglected the armed services were exposed for all to see. Much of the BEF could be evacuated, but its surviving tanks, its artillery and its heavy equipment would have to be left behind in France; nor could its remnants be re-equipped for several months to come. In purely military - if not in naval and air warfare - terms, the United Kingdom was temporarily defenceless if Hitler chose to invade after France, already tottering, had been beaten to her knees.

The possibility of invasion was taken very seriously indeed and contingency plans were laid in case the Government was forced to leave London quickly. These included the setting up of so-called H transmitters at important centres throughout the country. The H transmitters had a range of between five and fifteen miles and were normally used to rebroadcast the BBC Home Service in areas of poor reception. In the event of an emergency, they were immediately available to the Regional Commissioners or their representatives who would use them to make announcements, issue orders and keep the local population informed of developments. Liverpool's H transmitter was located in a single-storey building inside the factory of William Crawford and Sons, biscuit manufacturers, just off Edge Lane.

Even before the Dunkirk evacuation commenced the Cabinet had decided to transfer the national gold reserve from London to Liverpool. The strongroom of Martins' Bank, Water Street, was considered to be the most secure location since it was cut into the city's bedrock and its walls and roof were lined with concrete three feet thick, interlaced with iron bars, while its doors weighed nine tons. The arrangements were worked out jointly by the Bank of England and Martins' on a need-to-know basis and shortly before midnight on 22 May a special train, carrying 'boxes of unknown content', drew into Lime Street Station's No. 8 platform. The boxes, which weighed in total almost 100 tons, contained either bullion bars or gold sovereigns and took almost three hours to transfer to the waiting lorries. The convoy then set offfor Martins', travelling along Dale Street, the police having simply been told that a secret consignment would be using the route and that a slightly increased presence in the area of the Town Hall would be appreciated. In the narrow street between the Town Hall and Martins' was an escape hatch leading from the latter's air raid shelter to the pavement, and within this a chute had been erected. The chute had been borrowed from John Morrell and Company, provision merchants of Victoria Street, one of whose directors was also a local director of Martins', and was normally used for cheese and butter deliveries. Now, creaking and groaning, it carried the symbol of the nation's wealth for the next four hours. Further bullion shipments took place on the nights of 24 and 31 May, until the strongroom contained no less than 260 tons of gold, valued in 1940 at £750 million. In the later stages of the operation, the chute proved unequal to the continuous strain and several boxes fell to the ground, covering the stone floor with gleaming sovereigns.

Five weeks later the gold was loaded aboard the liner *Monarch of Bermuda,* which joined ships from the Clyde conveying further bullion consignments, including private stocks, previously sent to Glasgow. The convoy, escorted by the battleship HMS *Revenge,* the cruiser HMS *Bonaventure* and four destroyers, carried gold and securities valued at £1,250 million. On arrival in Halifax, Nova Scotia, the bullion was transported to the Bank of Canada's Head Office in Wellington Street, Ottawa. The directors of Martins' declined to make any charge for the Bank's services and later recorded the event with a small plaque on the wall of their building, close to the escape manhole; both plaque and manhole still exist.

The Bank of England's Liverpool branch also received consignments of bullion from public and private stocks during this period. The Bank's bullion yard had not yet been built and the deliveries followed the usual route of coin and note deliveries, through a security "window" off Cook Street. The Bank's archives contain a letter dated February 1940 seeking confirmation that 'the tail-board [of the lorry] can be placed close enough to the entrance so that the boxes can be lifted off onto the entrance sill without being placed on the ground'.

It has often been said that if Hitler had invaded the United Kingdom in the immediate aftermath of Dunkirk his troops would quickly have overrun the whole country. Such an invasion, fortunately, was impossible, as the Wehrmacht still had to deal with the surviving French armies before it could commence preparations for so large an operation and, in the meantime, week by week, the British Army gradually recovered its strength. The earliest practical date an invasion could have been launched was the last week of September. Its probable outcome was analysed by C.S. Forester, the creator of Captain Horatio Hornblower, in a short story published shortly after the end of the war, and it confirmed that while the German airborne and amphibious landings on the south coast would have succeeded, and even made some progress towards London, after several days their cross-Channel supply line would have been cut by the RAF and the Home Fleet with the result that the troops involved would have been isolated and forced to surrender.

This analysis was confirmed in 1974 when the *Daily Telegraph* and the Department of War Studies at the Royal Military Academy, Sandhurst, jointly sponsored a war game played by senior British and German officers in full possession of all the facts. The key element in both studies was the ability of the RAF to deny the Luftwaffe air superiority over southern England. If, in the summer of 1940, the RAF had lost that battle, the entire complexion of the campaign would have been radically altered, since without its support the Home Fleet would have been exposed to the same dive-bomber squadrons which later inflicted cruel losses on the Royal Navy off Crete, and the probability is that the German supply line would have remained intact. At times, the margin between success and failure was fearfully thin.

Had the Wehrmacht overrun the United Kingdom the Nazi hierarchy had already made thorough plans on how the country was to be governed. The officer who was to have been given overall responsibility for internal security was SS Standartenfahrer (Colonel) Professor Franz Six, described as 'short and bald, with ears that stuck out, and heavy pebble spectacles that inadequately concealed a pronounced squint'. From his London headquarters, Six was to have imposed his will through provincial offices set up in Birmingham, Bristol, Liverpool, Manchester and either Edinburgh or Glasgow. Liverpool, as the major transatlantic port, had been subjected to the attention of agents during the pre-war years and a full dossier existed on the city and its inhabitants.

Before 1914, there had been a substantial German community living in Liverpool, sufficient to support a Lutheran church in Renshaw Street. The residue of this had become naturalized, and the agents doubted whether it was remotely interested in providing direct support for the Fatherland's cause, deploring the fact that 'only a very few of their children speak a word of German'. Nor did the city's communists and discontented workers offer much cause for encouragement since, as one agent put it, 'these small groups exerted no influence'. Having gone to some trouble to cultivate a trade union leader, the same agent lost him following a monumental row over German involvement in the Spanish Civil War. Some assistance was anticipated from the Irish element of the population, and may indeed have been forthcoming in isolated cases. The Chinese and coloured communities were dismissed as being of no consequence. On the other hand, the agents found no difficulty in identifying their archenemy.

One wrote in his report:

> There are Jews everywhere in business and culture, among the teaching staff at the university and in the student body. I got to know a Jew who wanted to be an officer. *This was quite possible.* There was no sign of an anti-Semitic movement, although I was particularly on the look-out for it. Only occasionally did one hear a student say, 'I can't stand Jews.'

Had the Germans come to Liverpool the probability is that at first their policy would have been similar to that in Holland and the Channel Islands. They might have set up their headquarters in the Liver Buildings or India Buildings, both of which were very suitable for the purpose, the Adelphi Hotel would have become an officers' club, and the villas around Sefton Park would have been requisitioned for senior ranks, Party officials and, of course, the Gestapo. Their behaviour would have been absolutely correct and they would have been at pains to stress that the British and Germans were cousins and ancient allies whose tragic quarrel was now happily ended. To emphasize the point, the Union Flag and the Swastika would have been draped alternately from the columns of St George's Hall and other public buildings.

Subtly, the climate would have changed. Jews would

have been forbidden to hold public office or work in any of the professions; then their property would have been confiscated; then they would have vanished without trace or explanation, as would anyone who posed the slightest threat. Perhaps in Liverpool the relationship between conquerors and conquered would have deteriorated faster than anywhere else in the country, since the very act of talking back to authority, ingrained in its citizens, was utterly alien to the German sense of order and discipline. Acts of sabotage in the docks or on the railways would have been ruthlessly punished. The first attempt to strike would have been instantly crushed by the SS, who would shoot or hang indiscriminately and on the spot. The Gestapo's grip would have been total and, unpalatable as it may be, the fact is that its reign of terror would have been actively assisted by some members of the community. Among the grimmer reminders of the German occupation of the Channel Islands are Gestapo files of anonymous letters denouncing fellow-citizens guilty of some breach of regulations, written for reasons only intelligible to the senders, who must have been aware of the consequences; sadly, there is no evidence that human nature is any different in Liverpool than it is in Jersey or Guernsey.

For decent men holding public office, the arrival of the Germans would have presented an insoluble dilemma. On the one hand, their function was to serve the people, yet on the other it was they who would be made responsible for implementing German policy. As Sir Joseph Cleary, a future Lord Mayor then serving as a councillor, put it,

> I suppose the Council would have had to suffer or tolerate German occupation. We would need a structure of government, we would need our social services. In that context we would have gone on controlling the city to the best of our ability in the interest of the citizens. But I still feel that come what may, and no matter what the risk might have been, I could not have carried out policies which would have meant the deporting or executing of Jews or any other minority.

It was a path beset with terrible dangers.

Mercifully, the nightmare never became a reality, but people were aware of its nature. The prospect sent cold worms of fear wriggling through the intestines, but it also generated anger and fierce determination to resist. Throughout that fine summer, while the church bells hung silent, waiting to signal the coming of the invader, the nation achieved a unity of purpose unequalled in its history. While the armaments factories worked round the clock to replace the tanks and guns which the Army had been forced to abandon in France, the members of the Home Guard, many of them veterans of World War I, drilled the harder with their shotguns, pikes and broom handles, learned how to disable armoured vehicles with petrol bombs and crowbars, and prayed that if the moment came they would have something more substantial with which to fight the enemy. Nightly, families gathered round their radios to listen to the accounts of the day's air battles over southern England. Slowly, and with infinite relief, it was appreciated that, thanks to a comparative handful of very young and very tired fighter pilots, the threat of invasion was passing.

Thus far, Liverpool had escaped the Luftwaffe's attentions, but now that the enemy controlled the Channel coast it was generally accepted that the confrontation was imminent. Just what the German bombers could achieve had been demonstrated in September 1939, when they had torn the heart out of Warsaw, and in May 1940, when they had turned the commercial quarter of the port of Rotterdam into an inferno, hastening the surrender of the Dutch Government. Even as the Wehrmacht settled into its occupation duties, one senior and far-sighted German officer was recommending the total destruction of Liverpool as a means of persuading the Churchill administration to accept the Fuhrer's peace overtures.

3

Battle is Joined

The Wehrmacht's conquests during the spring and summer of 1940 provided the Luftwaffe with the means to strike at any target within the British Isles, for whereas formerly its long-range bombers had to fly from Germany itself, it now possessed a chain of airfields stretching from northern Norway to the Bay of Biscay. On 20 July 1940 it had three *Luftflotten* (Air Fleets) deployed in the West: Luftflotte 5 (Colonel-General Hans-Jurgen Stumpff), stationed in Norway and Denmark, with its headquarters in Oslo; Luftflotte 2 (Field Marshal Albert Kesseling), stationed in Holland, Belgium and northern France east of the Seine, with its headquarters in Brussels; and Luftflotte 3 (Field Marshal Hugo Sperrle), stationed in northern France west of the Seine, with its headquarters at St Cloud, near Paris. Luftflotte 5 could muster 129 long-range bombers, while together Luftflotten 2 and 3 could produce no less than 1,131.

Liverpool's principal enemy was to be Sperrle's Luftflotte 3. Very few German officers actually resembled the film and cartoon caricatures used by the Allied propaganda apparatus to portray them, but Sperrle was a notable exception, being thick-set, bull-necked, heavily jowled and be-monocled; furthermore, he pursued the sumptuous lifestyle which he believed appropriate to a conquering field marshal and requisitioned the Palais de Luxembourg for his own use. He was, nonetheless, an able commander and had his advice been heeded the Battle of Britain would have been conducted in a more realistic manner.

The long-range bombers available to the Luftwaffe included the four-seater Dornier Do 17Z, with a maximum speed of 265 mph and a 2,205-lb (1000-kilo) bomb load; the five-seater Heinkel He 111, with a maximum speed of 255 mph and a 4,410-lb (2,000-kilo) bomb load; and the six-seater Junkers Ju 88, with a maximum speed of 286 mph and a bomb load of up to 6,614-lb (3,000 kilo). These were all twin-engined aircraft, the engines of which had been deliberately desynchronized to distort the reception of the British sound locators; they had an operational ceiling of between 25,500 and 26,500 feet and were armed with several machine guns for strafing and their immediate defence. When maximum effort was required they could be supplemented by the Focke-Wulf Fw 200, a four-engined maritime reconnaissance and anti-shipping aircraft, designed originally as a commercial air liner, which had a maximum speed of 224 mph and carried a 4,626-lb (2,100-kilo) bomb load.

The bombs most commonly carried were general purpose high-explosive 50, 250 and 500 kilos, which produced craters, respectively, of up to fifteen, twentyfive and thirty feet across, but larger bombs of up to 1,800 kilos were sometimes used. There were also several types of incendiary bomb, the most common being the one kilo, dropped in clusters from canisters. The 250-kilo incendiary was known as an oil bomb and was filled with oil which was spread by a high-explosive bursting charge; the 500-kilo incendiary contained a much greater high-explosive content. The twelve-kilo fragmentation bomb was an anti-personnel weapon intended to cause casualties with its splinter effect. Another anti-personnel device was the butterfly bomb, which weighed two kilos and was fitted with wings like a sycamore seed to retard its descent. The butterfly bomb was deliberately painted in bright colours to attract children and the curious, and would explode instantly if handled, causing death or fatal injury within a twenty-five-yard radius, the object being demoralization of the civil population. Most feared of all were the so-called land mines, which exploded with a devastating blast effect and could create craters up to eighty feet in diameter. These were actually sea mines, and as far as Liverpool was concerned were intended for use in the river and the approach channels to the port, but they were parachute-dropped and often carried inland by the prevailing wind. The two principal types were the 500-kilo LMA and the 1,000-kilo LMB III. They were often dropped during the course of a general raid but were also laid during specific missions flown by the Luftwaffe's *Kuestenfliegergruppen* (Coastal Air Groups).

Navigational aids employed by the Luftwaffe included the *Knickebein* (bent leg) directional radio beam, which worked through the aircraft's standard Lorenz radio receiver. The beam was directed from the transmitter directly at the target. If the aircraft flew to the left of the beam, the receiver gave out a series of dots; if it flew to the right the signal was a series of dashes; on the beam itself the tone was continuous. Above the target a second radio beam intersected the first, the combined tone informing the crew that the moment had come to release their bombs. By the end of August 1940 twelve *Knickebein* transmitters were functioning.

Rather more sophisticated was the *X-Geraet* (X-apparatus). This employed four radio beams, one pointed directly at the target, intersected by three more, one fifty kilometres (thirty-one miles) short of the bomb release point, the second twenty kilometres (12½ miles) short, and the third five kilometres (three miles) short, the appropriate warning being given at each intersection. The device was used in conjunction with a clock which triggered bomb release automatically. More complex still was the *Y-Geraet,* which enabled ground operators to plot the aircraft's position in relation to the previously calculated bomb release point, at which the crew received the order to bomb. The device was technically advanced and, after its early faults had been rectified, became fully operational in January 1941.

The *X*- and *Y-Geraet* required the fitting of special sets and the training of operators in their use, and were thus unsuitable for general issue. It was decided, therefore, to form special Pathfinder units which, with their electronic assistance, would locate the target accurately and start marker fires on which the rest of the raiders would converge. The most famous of these Pathfinder units was KG (*Kampfgruppe* or Battle Group) 100, but KG 26 was also trained and employed in the role.

One problem encountered with radio-beam navigation was that the beams became progressively weaker the further they travelled from the transmitter. Another was that British scientists had evolved their own electronic counter-measures. These included transmitting decoy beams which led nowhere, and in 'bending' the genuine beams. The battle of the beams, coupled with the Starfish decoy fires, certainly made life more difficult for the bomber crews, but in the final analysis Luftflotte 3's route to Liverpool from its airfields in Normandy and Brittany was signposted all the way and the target itself was easily identified unless completely obscured by cloud. The bombers flew over south-western England, then crossed the Bristol Channel to St David's Head where they turned due north to cross Cardigan Bay, then east-north-east over Anglesey for the last leg of the journey. The route had the advantage that it lay clear of anti-aircraft defences almost all the way, while to the west the distant lights of neutral Dublin enabled navigators to check their position. Having dropped their bombs, the raiders would return home the same way.

In November 1939 Luftwaffe Intelligence had stressed the importance of maintaining heavy attacks on the major British ports, emphasizing that the proximity of residential property to the docklands was to be ignored. The primary objective was stated as being shipping, with the docks, warehouses and handling facilities as secondary targets. This curious allocation of priorities reflected the strictly compartmentalized approach of the

German services, for the destruction of shipping could be achieved far more efficiently by the Navy's U-boat arm, while the elimination of the dockland facilities by the Luftwaffe would yield much greater benefits in the longer term. Later that month Hitler issued his War Directive No. 9, entitled *Instructions For Warfare Against the Economy of the Enemy.* The essence of the directive was that once the Channel coast had been secured following the defeat of the Allied armies in Western Europe, the Navy and the Luftwaffe were to mine and block the approaches to the major British ports and destroy their installations, including oil, food and grain stores and lock gates. Liverpool was specifically identified as being a target of'decisive importance'.

Hitler took some pride in his grasp of economic warfare and was much given to passing unjustifiable comments on his generals' ignorance of the subject. The truth was that he often allowed his own economic objectives to become obscured by the purely military considerations of the moment, and in the excitement of his conquests in Poland, Norway, Holland, Belgium and France, Liverpool was forgotten. Furthermore, the majority of his senior officers were land animals and unlikely to remind him of the port on the United Kingdom's west coast, far removed from the seat of war. The exception was Grand Admiral Erich Raeder, the Commander-in-Chief of the German Navy. Raeder was fully aware of British weakness in the immediate aftermath of Dunkirk, but he had serious reservations regarding the outcome of Operation Sea Lion, Hitler's projected invasion of the United Kingdom, not the least of which stemmed from the Navy's sharp reduction in strength following recent heavy losses off Norway. This was, however, the period which U-boat commanders would look back on as their Happy Time, for in June alone they sent 355,000 tons of Allied shipping to the bottom, and Raeder was confident that, under the direction of Admiral Karl Doenitz, the U-boats could effect a slow strangulation of Britain's lifeline. Nevertheless, he felt that the process of collapse could be accelerated and in July he urged Hitler to employ the combined strength of Luftflotten 2 and 3 in a concentrated bomber offensive against Liverpool, the object being nothing less than the destruction of the port itself so that even those cargoes which did arrive could not be handled. Once Liverpool had been destroyed, he argued, the British capacity to wage war, and indeed to survive, would be so reduced that the Churchill Government would be more receptive to peace offers. Furthermore, the adoption of such a strategy would remove the need for Sea Lion, and with it the numerous risks entailed.

Raeder's indirect solution to the problem of British intransigence had much to command it and, given the combined strength of Luftflotten 2 and 3, lay well within the German capacity to implement quickly. Whether it would have had the effect Raeder anticipated remains an open question, but it is worth recalling that the final collapse of the Third Reich itself stemmed directly from a major air offensive which destroyed Germany's internal communications, so severing the link between the armaments factories and the various fronts.

Fortunately for the United Kingdom, Hitler was not prepared to take Raeder's excellent advice, and the reason for this lay in the rivalries and personal animosities which existed in the upper echelons of the Nazi hierarchy. Hermann Goering, Reichsmarschall, Chief Huntsman of Germany and Head of the Luftwaffe, was close to the Fuhrer and there was little love lost between him and Raeder. Moreover, he intended regaining the face he had lost in failing to prevent the evacuation of the British Expeditionary force from the Dunkirk beaches and he was determined to persevere in his attempts to gain mastery of the air above southern England as a prerequisite to Sea Lion. In the circumstances, therefore, he was totally unreceptive to the idea of an alternative bomber offensive planned by the Navy.

Once Fighter Command had contained his initial onslaught, however, Goering seemed unable to evolve a coherent strategy. The essence of his tactical difficulty was that his own fighters' limited fuel endurance prevented them from remaining with the bombers they were meant to escort to and from the target areas, and in consequence the latter sustained serious losses. Understandably, the bomber crews complained and, in order to minimize the rate of attrition, the Luftwaffe began to drift towards a policy of night bombing. During the night of 24/25 August bombs were, accidentally and quite contrary to orders, dropped on London. The following night the RAF retaliated by bombing Berlin, provoking an emotional response from Hitler and Goering. This took the form of a sustained bomber offensive directed against London, and the devastation caused in the capital's docklands served to emphasize the crucial importance of Liverpool to the national survival. Other centres of population were also attacked, but the net result was that the hard-pressed Fighter Command was able to recover its balance and inflict yet further losses. By mid-September it was clear that the Luftwaffe could neither obtain air superiority nor break British civilian morale. On the 18th, with autumn gales in the Channel a probability, Sea Lion was postponed indefinitely and the invasion force was dispersed.

Hitler now turned his attention elsewhere and began to prepare for the invasion of the Soviet Union, codenamed Barbarossa. The destruction of the cradle of Communism was a long-cherished ambition and he believed that the Wehrmacht had 'only to kick in the door and the whole rotten house would come tumbling down'. With Russia out of the way, he reasoned, the United States would be less inclined to send further aid to the British, and Churchill would be compelled to accept the futility of continuing the war. This, then, was the background against which Liverpool sustained its first air attacks.

The Luftwaffe had, in fact, been visiting Merseyside intermittently since 25 June when, shortly after midnight, the warning sirens gave the Alert in earnest for the first time. Rising and falling, the sound was eerie, pregnant with menace, and could cause the hairs to rise on the back of one's neck; after a while, one hated it for its own sake as much as for its implications. Against its background people rose from their beds, collected a few belongings and hurried to their shelters. The Main Control Room at Belmont Hospital was activated, the Fire Brigade and Civil Defence teams stood to and soldiers ran to man their anti-aircraft guns and searchlights. The sirens stopped. Soon, the undulating hum of desynchronized aircraft engines could be heard approaching. In silence, people waited for the first shock of screaming bombs, explosions and the thump of the guns, but there was nothing. Then, the noise began to fade and was followed by the sirens sounding the All Clear, long and steady like the dawn of a new day. It had all been a tremendous anticlimax.

Almost certainly, the intruder was engaged on a reconnaissance mission and, finding the area obscured by cloud, had simply turned for home. Similar missions, some armed with bombs, were flown on 2, 15, 16, 22, 24 and 29 July and 1 August. The anti-aircraft guns went into action, rattling the windows, and although bombs were dropped and some damage caused, there were as yet no casualties. Most of the comparatively few bombs dropped fell in fields on the Wirral or on farmland on the outskirts of Liverpool, and people went out to examine the craters. Sooner or later, however, it was inevitable that even random bombing such as this would find its mark in built-up areas. On 9 August a stick of bombs ploughed through Prenton. One crashed through the roof of a house in Prenton Lane, where a maid named Johanna Mandale was killed instantly while she slept. Perhaps she was unaware that a raid was in progress or perhaps, like many, she had begun to underestimate the danger. Whatever the truth, her name was tragically to head Merseyside's civilian Roll of Honour. The following night four more were to die and four sustain serious injury when bombs were unloaded over Wallasey.

This low-level activity, accompanied by aerial minelaying in the approaches to the river, continued for the rest of the month. In purely military terms, much of it was mere nuisance value, although during the night of 17/18 August a small number of bombs hit Brunswick, North Coburg and South Queen's docks, damaging a grain silo, the London, Midland and Scottish Railway's goods depot and part of the Overhead Railway. In Brunswick Dock itself a near miss stove in the hull of the Dock Board's bucket dredger *Lyster,* which turned turtle and sank; salvage work commenced immediately.

During the uproar which followed the bombing of Berlin, Goering ordered Luftflotte 3 to mount a series of *Grossangriffen* (major attacks in which not less than 199 tons of high explosive were dropped) against Liverpool at the end of August. This did not represent a conversion to Raeder's views, since London remained the major target, and the intention was simply to demonstrate that the Luftwaffe could fly where it liked and inflict heavy damage whenever it chose to. The maximum effort was demanded from Sperrle's command and during the last four nights of August it despatched respectively 160, 176, 148, and 145 bombers against Liverpool. Of these 629 sorties, the crews of 448 aircraft reported that they had dropped no less than 456 tons of high explosive and 1,029 incendiary canisters directly onto the target area.

The truth was rather different and had Sperrle and his staff known it they would have been less than pleased with the result of their efforts. The fact was that, with the exception of the fourth night, Merseysiders were quite unaware that they had been selected for special attention. During the first three nights casualties and damage had been caused, notably at Mossley Hill Church, but, thanks to the "bending" of directional radio beams and the use of decoys, most of the bomb loads had been scattered uselessly on the Welsh mountains. On the night of 31 August/1 September, however, the bombers found their target. Wallasey Town Hall was extensively damaged, as was warehouse property in Stone and Vandares Streets, the Customs House was set ablaze and 100 minor fires broke out. One incident of which neither the enemy nor the British public knew anything was that the ill-fated King George V Class battleship *Prince of*

Wales, then fitting out in the wet basin of Cammel Laird's shipyard, was seriously damaged when a bomb burst between the ship and the wall of her berth, rupturing the hull and causing her to list dangerously as thousands of tons of water poured aboard. While divers patched the damaged plating she was pumped out by the Birkenhead Fire Brigade in an operation lasting 2½ days, then moved to dry dock and made ready for sea.

Further attacks, of comparatively minor intensity, took place during September, October and most of November, delivered at an average frequency of one every other night. These added to the growing toll of dead, seriously injured and homeless, but, despite extensive damage to property, had little effect on the daily life of the city or the running of the port. Rather, by beginning its attacks on Merseyside in a low key, the Luftwaffe forfeited the shock element of a major offensive, so that when the time for heavier raids came the population were psychologically prepared and the Civil Defence organizations had eliminated most of the snags in their operational procedures.

It was during this period, too, that a marvellous spirit of comradeship evolved, born of dangers, sorrows and losses equally shared. The bombs fell impartially on old and young, rich and poor, Protestant and Catholic. Such differences meant nothing to the Luftwaffe and they quickly ceased to mean anything on the ground. Grief at the sudden and terrible loss of a loved one was as sharp and painful whether one lived in Scotland Road, Toxteth, Woolton, or anywhere else. It hurt everyone equally to return from the shelter and find that their home had been blown apart, then to have to pick through the rubble to salvage a few possessions. It required the coldest of hearts to walk past a house damaged beyond repair, see the sad litter of broken furniture, torn curtains and treasured nick-nacks, the accumulation of someone's lifetime, and not know fellow-feeling. Suddenly, old prejudices, jealousies, enmities and feuds seemed stupid and irrelevant. People helped each other in a thousand ways, without being asked; often, bombed-out neighbours would receive gifts of clothing and furniture to start them off in their new life. It was a measure of the time that looting was virtually unknown.

There were, however, two things which annoyed the people of Liverpool very much. The first was that in September 1940 an alteration in the licensing laws required pubs to close at 9 p.m. In the final analysis this made very little difference, partly because the Luftwaffe was already interrupting serious drinking on a regular basis, and partly because there was a general shortage of supplies, but it was felt in many quarters that the new regulations were an unwarranted imposition; not until October 1943 was the situation eased, and then by only thirty minutes. The second was the BBC's reporting of the Luftwaffe's attacks on Merseyside, which was never referred to by name, but always under the more general heading of the North West, while attacks on London were fully reported. Everyone knew that London was taking a tremendous hammering, and no one begrudged Londoners every credit for standing up to it in so exemplary a fashion, but that was no reason to avoid mentioning Liverpool's share in the war. The somewhat lame excuse was that the Blitz on London could hardly be concealed from the world, but that it was in the national interest not to specify that a critically important target like Liverpool was being hit regularly by the enemy. Since the enemy were not fools, and Luftflotte 3 knew exactly what was happening, the exercise of such discretion was pointless.

In fact, bomb-aiming was still a far-from-exact science and the enemy was hitting very little of military or economic significance. On the night of 5/6 September a major conflagration engulfed the premises of the Liverpool Grease, Oil and Chemical Company in Norfolk Street and much of the stained glass in the Cathedral was blown in. During the night of 18/19 September a bomb demolished a wing of Walton Prison, killing a number of prisoners. When the rubble was cleared twenty-one bodies were removed, but one man remained unaccounted for. The Governor was convinced that he had escaped, but eleven years later his remains were discovered on the site of the building. Two nights later Central Station was penetrated and rolling stock wrecked. Simultaneously, major fires were started in warehouses at the Alexandra Dock and in Byng Street, as well as in a timber yard at Rimrose Road, Bootle. That same night my father, then serving as a Special Constable, was standing outside T.J. Hughes's department store in London Road when the building was struck by a heavy bomb; he regained consciousness in the doorway of a rival concern, Collier's, having been blown seventy-five yards across Pembroke Place without so much as hearing the explosion.

On 24/25 September warehouses in Great Howard Street and Love Lane sustained damage and fires were started in the shopping areas of Clayton Square and Church Street. It was not, however, until the night of the 26/27 that Luftflotte 3 managed to deliver what, in its own terms, could be described as an effective attack. Widespread damage was caused in the area of Wapping, King's, Queen's, Coburg and Brunswick Docks, destroying thirteen warehouses and the Admiralty Stores in Canning Place. The Dock Board and Cunard offices were hit but the fires started within were quickly contained; among the water-damaged items salvaged from the latter were boxed medals commemorating the *Queen Mary's* first transatlantic crossing. The tug *Wellington,* berthed on the knuckle between King's Nos 1 and 2 Docks, was set ablaze and further damaged when the wall of a burning building collapsed onto her deck; she was towed out in a sinking condition and beached, but was later refloated and repaired. In Birkenhead the world-famous Argyll Theatre was gutted by fire. In the LMS/GWR marshalling yard at Birkenhead three railwaymen, Shunter Norman Tunna, Driver Ivor Thomas and Fireman Frank Newns, became the first Merseyside civilians to be decorated for gallantry. The ammunition train they were manning was struck by incendiary bombs which, when the tarpaulins were removed from the wagons, were found burning among the cargo of stacked high-explosive bombs. All three knew that an explosion of horrific proportions was probable, but they set to without thought for their own safety, Newns manning a stirrup pump while Thomas levered the heavy bombs apart and Tunna removed the blazing incendiaries. Thanks to their efforts, the train was saved, and many lives with it. Tunna received the George Cross, the civilian equivalent of the Victoria Cross, and Thomas and Newns the George Medal.

By the end of September 327 Merseysiders had been killed and 590 seriously injured by enemy action. Further light raids continued throughout October, with 136 killed and 167 seriously injured added to the growing total and, week by week, more wrecked homes, damaged warehouses and gutted factories. Occasionally, daylight reconnaissance intruders would make strafing runs at suitable targets, as at Speke airfield on 3 October. On the nearby main road was a bus carrying women factory workers, the driver of which believed his vehicle was the target and took fierce evasive action before delivering his charges safely to the nearest air raid shelter. Whatever the Germans' intentions, the driver behaved with courage and skill, although the story grew somewhat in the telling by his excited passengers. One said the attack was made by a 'three-engined bomber', although, with the exception of a few seaplanes, the only tri-motor in Luftwaffe service was the Junkers Ju 52 transport, which did not appear over Liverpool; another that the machine-gun bullets could be heard 'spattering' the roof of the bus; and, for good measure, that a watching fireman had had his hat shot off. Such tales were legion; they did no harm, and perhaps they even did some good.

The Luftwaffe was also sustaining casualties in its forays over Liverpool. The Anti-Aircraft Command Intelligence Report for 24 September records that at 0251 hours Mersey 1 Gunsite engaged a Dornier Do 17 and at the second salvo of 3.7-inch shells the aircraft began to lose height and, despite attempts to level out, burst into flames and plunged into the sea. On 8 October three Hurricanes of 312 Squadron, flying from Speke, bounced a lone Ju 88 intruder and forced it to crash-land near Bromborough, the entire engagement from take-off to touch-down lasting less than eight minutes. Such events encouraged the civil population but, as mentioned previously, most fighter interceptions took place many miles from Liverpool. For example, during the evening of 11 October the Spitfires of 611 (West Lancashire) Squadron, flying from Tern Hill, had the satisfaction of tangling with Liverpool-bound Do 17Zs of *Kuestenfliegergruppe* 606 over Caernarvon, and a fierce air battle developed. This resulted in one Dornier shot down in the sea off Anglesey, another sharing a similar fate off the Lleyn Peninsula, and a third crashing near Capel Curig; a fourth kill, shared with 312 Squadron's Hurricanes, went down near Chester, and a fifth Do 17Z was so badly damaged that two of its crew baled out before it managed to crash-land near Brest. The RAF's casualties amounted to one Spitfire and one Hurricane damaged. There were, of course, other interceptions and a steady trickle of Luftflotte 3's aircraft were limping home, riddled by flak or fighters, with dead and wounded aboard, although on average Sperrle's command was sustaining an acceptable casualty rate of between one and four per cent which could be sustained indefinitely. Equally, the Luftwaffe had barely scratched Liverpool's capacity to survive.

This indecisive skirmishing continued into the following month, but on the night of 28/29 November there occurred an incident which Churchill later described as being one of the worst of the entire war. It was certainly a night I am unlikely forget. Our family home was then a tall Victorian house, the wine cellar of which had been reinforced with heavy timbers until it resembled a World War I dugout. It had been made extremely snug and, if the worst happened and the house was hit, there was an escape route up the chute of the adjoining coal cellar. I was then six and being woken to go down to the shelter had ceased to be an adventure. From the adults' reactions I quickly learned which sounds were dangerous and which were not. The scream of near-misses was piercing and personal enough to make everyone duck, but the whistle of more distant sticks of bombs was flatter and could be disregarded. That night, for several hours, there were only the usual sounds of battle aircraft engines, the continuous thumping of the guns, the howl of bombs, explosions, the ringing of fire engine and ambulance bells, and sometimes urgent shouts from the road outside. Then, at 0155 there was a thunderous explosion like the crack of doom. There was the sound of smashing glass and a series of crashes from above. Plaster dust showered through cracks between the reinforcement beams and the electric light bulb swung on its flex. Nobody seemed to move for many minutes of what seemed like comparative silence, although outside the uproar continued as before. At length, someone went to inspect the damage. The house was still standing, but all the glass at the front had been blown in; the heavy front door had been ripped off its hinges, as had the inner vestibule door, and both lay in the hall.

After a while, there was the noise of feet crunching on glass above and the cellar door opened.

'You all right down there?'

It was Eric Haigh, the curate of St Cyprian's Church, who, like the rest of the clergy, regarded himself as being on duty whatever the Luftwaffe was doing, and was to be found dropping in on parishioners in their shelters, or helping in any way he was able, often in circumstances of extreme danger.

'The shelter in Durning Road has been hit. Can you look after these people until the attack's over?'

We said we could and they came down the cellar steps, perhaps six or eight of them. They were a terrible sight. They were staggering with shock, their clothes were torn and they were covered from head to foot in brick and plaster dust. There was dust in their hair, ingrained in their skin, and their eyes were red-raw with it; one or two were unable to see until the grime was washed out with water. Some had serious cuts and abrasions which also needed cleaning, the black congealed blood having already mingled with the dirt. They sat silently, huddled in blankets, their teeth chattering and their hands shaking as they tried to drink hot tea. At length, a woman began to cry, softly.

'There were hundreds in there,'she said. 'Hundreds.'

'Don't worry,' said her husband. 'They'll get them out. They got us out, didn't they?'

Bit by bit, they told their story. When the raid began they had been riding on two trams which had stopped outside the Ernest Brown Junior Technical School in Durning Road. The basement of the school had been converted into a large public shelter and they had sought refuge there. The shelter was very crowded and they had only been able to find places near the door. Beyond that, all they knew was that there had been a tremendous explosion and the three-storey building above had collapsed into the basement, burying everyone. The rescue teams had dug them out fairly quickly, but for anyone further inside the shelter the outlook was grim.

The All Clear sounded at 0400 and, as soon as they felt fit enough to move, our visitors left. We saw them off at the front gate and by then their spirits had returned somewhat.

'Thanks a lot - you've been very kind. Maybe we can do the same for you some day!'

'Let's hope you don't have to!'

'Aye, right enough! Cheerio, then!'

In one man fierce anger suddenly welled to the surface. He thanked us, then, looking back at our doorless, windowless house with curtains and blackout material hanging in tatters within, pointed at the sky.

'They won't get away with it, you know! We'll get them for what they've done to us! Our turn's coming, make no mistake about it - then we'll see how they like it!'

We all knew that something terrible had happened, but the full extent of the tragedy did not become apparent until the next day. As well as bombs, the raiders had dropped thirty parachute mines, but the majority of these had drifted inland and exploded in the suburbs, with devastating effect. It was one of these which had landed on the Junior Technical School. Many of the 290 people in the shelter died instantly. The lights failed and, to add to the horror, the contents of the school's furnaces started a fire in the debris, filling the interior with choking smoke. As if this was not bad enough, a boiler and water main burst, filling the basement to knee level. The real heroine of the night was an Air Raid Warden, Mrs F.B. Taft, who calmed the survivors and then began a methodical search in the hot, crowded, asphyxiating darkness for a way out. At length she discovered a small window that had not been blocked by debris and someone flashed a torch through the aperture, attracting the rescue services. Despite desperately hard work, the last of the living was not brought out for two days, and by then the full horror of what had taken place was clearly revealed; 164 people had died in the shelter, and 96 had sustained serious injury. Only twenty or so, including our visitors, had emerged relatively unscathed. Most of the blast had gone one way, flattening several houses on the opposite side of Durning Road. Details of the tragedy were suppressed by the censor for a while and even photographs of the rescue teams at work were not passed for publication until 1943.

Eight of the parachute mines dropped that night failed to explode and were defused. One of them penetrated the No. 1 holder at Garston gas works. Employees of the gas company, assisted by the Fire Brigade, volunteered for the dangerous task of emptying the holder of its explosive contents. Then the Naval Mine Disposal Officer, Lieutenant Howard Newgass, RNVR, entered the holder through a hole cut in the roof. Wearing breathing apparatus, he worked for three hours save for brief spells to change his oxygen tanks, first securing the mine and then turning it so that he could remove the fuse, magnetic primer and clock. For his cool courage he received the immediate award of the George Cross.

For the next three weeks the Luftwaffe to all intents and purposes left Liverpool alone, but on 20 December Luftflotte 3 initiated a short series of raids which were to kill 702 people and inflict the heaviest damage yet. The first raid started numerous fires along the docks, as well as in the Dock Board and Cunard Buildings, the Town Hall, the Municipal Buildings and the Central Police

Office. A parachute mine exploded in Copperas Hill, severely damaging the north wing of the Adelphi Hotel. The worst event of the night occurred in Bentinck Street, where the railway viaduct carrying the line north from Exchange Station received a direct hit. The viaduct's arches were used by many people as shelters and forty-two were killed when the structure's heavy concrete blocks collapsed onto them; the size of the blocks presented the rescuers with a difficult problem and the last of forty-eight survivors was not pulled clear for two days. Exchange Station remained isolated for three months until repairs were completed over three months later; commuters using the Southport, Ormskirk and Wigan lines travelled between Exchange and Sandhills stations by means of bus and tram. In Huskisson Dock the 10,224-ton liner *Europa,* with six aircraft aboard, was severely holed when a hopper barge alongside was sunk by a bomb, and herself settled by the head; she was refloated and moved to Brocklebank graving dock where, in May 1941, she was so seriously damaged by fire that she became a constructive total loss, and was later beached for breaking up. During the same raid the 10,455-ton tanker *John A. Brown,* at anchor in the river, was hit by a bomb on her starboard side and was then severely damaged by a mine, losing about 700 tons of her cargo. She was moved to Dingle Oil jetty, where the rest of the cargo was discharged, and was subsequently repaired.

The following night's raids were even heavier, lasting from 1848 until 2040 and from midnight until 0515. Gladstone, Canada, Brocklebank, Prince's and King's Docks, together with their adjacent warehouses, all sustained serious damage and fires. In the Anfield district seventy-four people died when their shelter received a direct hit. At the Pier Head the famous parish church of Our Lady and St Nicholas was completely burned out, only the walls and the tower remaining. Some of the law courts within St George's Hall were also destroyed, but the building itself was saved. In Roe Street, the seven-man crew of a fire engine were killed when their vehicle drove into a bomb crater. Nearby, St John's Fish Market, well stocked with poultry for Christmas, was burning fiercely, the smell of roasting turkey providing a mouth-watering but bizarre distraction for those fighting more fires in the area. Hospitals, too, were hit hard, including the Royal Infirmary and Mill Road Infirmary. For the second night running reinforcement fire brigades arrived from far afield to assist in containing the damage, and Lancashire County Constabulary sent thirty men to support the hard pressed local force. A delayed-action bomb blew a large breach in the bank of the Liverpool and Leeds Canal and a torrent of water, bearing with it a coal barge, swept through to flood the LMS Canada Dock Goods Station. Several barges and flats were sunk in the docks, but these were raised and repaired. Not so the little freighter *Silvio,* which received a direct hit in Alexandra Dock and was considered unrepairable; nor the tug *Poolgarth,* so badly damaged when she struck a mine in the river that her remains were cut up for scrap. The 7,403-ton tanker *Elax,* in ballast, also struck a mine and was beached in a sinking condition. Refloated with the aid of salvage pumps, she was moved to Bidston Dock, Birkenhead, where she sustained further damage in March while awaiting repair.

On 22/23 December the Luftwaffe raided Merseyside and Manchester simultaneously, the latter absorbing the main weight of the attack, although dock and private property on both sides of the river sustained further damage. In Wallasey most of the residents of a women's home were killed when the building was hit; those that survived the impact itself were asphyxiated beneath the rubble by a ruptured gas main. A fourth raid was made the next night but achieved very poor results, some bombs landing in the river and others being scattered over the Welsh mountains.

If Luftflotte 3 had made a maximum effort during its series of pre-Christmas raids, so too had Merseyside. The Liverpool Corporation Passenger Transport Department, for example, commended those of its employees who had spent the nights serving as voluntary drivers for the fire, rescue and emergency feeding services yet still turned up for their normal turns of duty the following morning. In passing, the same meeting recorded that the cost of repairing tramway track and overhead cables damaged by enemy action during the period September-December 1940 amounted to £4,050.

In his memoirs, General Sir Frederick Pile, the Head of Anti-Aircraft Command, recorded:

> It was Merseyside that, on December 20/21, received the first of the really prolonged provincial attacks. For four nights the attack continued, and, although this may not seem great in comparison with such raids as had been pounding London for 75 nights, the difference in size of the two targets meant that the provincial centres suffered a disproportionately great concentration of damage. In Liverpool, where an outer barrage was immediately followed by an inner barrage, aimed fire by means of radar sets seemed to be more successful than it was in London.

For all that, Luftwaffe losses incurred during raids mounted 20 - 22 December amounted to only seven aircraft, with perhaps twice that number damaged to a greater or lesser degree. Again, while it was clear that since his defeat in the Battle of Britain, Goering had had no coherent strategy for his air offensive against the United Kingdom, at the tactical level Luftflotte 3 was beginning to develop some skill in its attacks on Liverpool. Evidence of this was provided by the number of ships damaged by mines which had been laid in the Mersey approaches during the December raids. On 27 December the Isle of Man Steam Packet Company's ferry *Victoria* struck a mine eight miles north-west of the Bar Lightship, the explosion leaving her dead in the water. Ships stood by her for several hours until HMS *Michael Griffith,* a requisitioned minesweeping trawler, managed to get a line aboard and tow her back into port. Nearby, the 2,284-ton cargo and passenger liner *Lady Connaught* also struck a mine and began taking in water; she was kept afloat with the aid of salvage pumps and brought in safely. Next day, it was the turn of the *Lochee,* with cased petrol aboard, which was similarly saved. *Catrine,* carrying bulk grain, was brought in on the 29th with mine damage; some of her cargo was saved, although the rest was spoiled by water, and the vessel itself sustained additional bomb damage in March 1941 while awaiting repair in Bidston Dock. On 31 December the 5,646-ton freighter *Buenos Aires,* making water and abandoned by her crew, was brought in and later repaired. On 15 January the little collier *Karri* struck a mine near the Bar; a fire which broke out forward was extinguished and, with the assistance of pumps, she reached port. Close to the Bar itself the steam hopper barge *Mancunium* sustained fatal damage and went down. The last casualty of this series of minings was the 9,496-ton freighter *Westmoreland,* with general cargo, rescued on 29 January.

Bad flying weather characterized the first two months of 1941. There were periodic visits by enemy reconnaissance flights but few raids, and none of any real intensity, although damage was inflicted on Herculaneum Dock and the Dingle Oil Depot. Total casualties for the two months were extremely light in view of what had gone before, amounting to fifty-five killed and forty-eight seriously injured.

Early in 1941 Churchill recognized that the country was now so dependent on the Mersey and the Clyde that 'it would seem that the problem constitutes the most dangerous part of our whole front'. Because German aircraft, surface raiders and U-boats were operating from the French coast, transatlantic convoys were being routed round the north of Ireland and for this reason Headquarters Western Approaches Command transferred from Plymouth to Liverpool on 7 February. The new headquarters, which became known as the Fortress, was established under several feet of reinforced concrete below the Derby House wing of Exchange Buildings. The headquarters contained a huge operations room with direct links to the Admiralty. It reproduced the London

Trade Plot, which showed details of merchant shipping movements, and received a constant flow of information from the Navy's Operational Intelligence Centre and Submarine Tracking Room, the Air Ministry and, of course, the top-secret Ultra source. Located within the same complex was the headquarters of the RAF's No. 15 Group Coastal Command which moved from Plymouth at the same time, first under Air Vice-Marshal J.M. Robb and later under Air Vice-Marshal Sir Leonard Slatter. The combined headquarters was the nerve centre of anti-submarine operations and so much depended on its survival that its facilities were duplicated underground within Lord Derby's estate at Knowsley. Subordinate to HQ Western Approaches was the Liverpool Sub-Command, the headquarters of which were in the Liver Buildings, with an area of responsibility stretching from the Scottish coast to Bardsey Island.

The task of the Commander-in-Chief Western Approaches, Admiral Sir Martin Dunbar-Nasmith, was as demanding as it was difficult. On his shoulders rested the responsibility of ensuring the arrival of the convoys upon which the nation's survival depended, despite the critical shortage of escort vessels; many had been lost during the Dunkirk evacuation and, although fifty old American destroyers had been acquired, there were never enough escorts to go round. He recognized the need to establish permanent escort groups which were used to working together and were familiar with every aspect of their work, and his ideas were adopted by his successor, Admiral Sir Percy Noble, who relieved him on 17 February. Noble set up anti-submarine warfare schools at Dunoon and Campbeltown and a sea-training establishment for newly commissioned escort vessels at Tobermory. Later, he formed support groups which would join a threatened convoy and hunt detected U-boats to destruction, leaving the escort groups free to continue their work.

March brought better weather and with it the Luftwaffe returned, delivering a heavy raid on the night of 12/13th. There was extensive damage and loss of life in

Wallasey and Birkenhead, and in Liverpool no less than 126 fires were started. The Cotton Exchange, the White Star Building, the Municipal Annexe in Dale Street and the General Post Office in Victoria Street all sustained serious damage; the top storey of the last was burned out and has never been renewed. Six firemen were killed and more were injured when a burning building was again struck by a high-explosive bomb. In Birkenhead's West Float the world-famous floating crane *Mammoth*, the largest in the Dock Board's fleet with a lifting capacity of 200 tons, was hit by two bombs and sank. Fortunately, she settled on an even keel and her immense jib remained intact; even so, seventeen months were to pass before she was returned to duty, and then only at a cost of £21,500. Mines dropped in the West Float also damaged two cargo vessels, the 6,278-ton *Myrmidon* with Government stores aboard, and the 5,691-ton *Empire Simba* with a cargo of steel; the former actually sank, although she was subsequently refloated and repaired, while the latter was kept afloat with pumps until she could be patched. In the river itself mines sank the 4,738-ton freighter *Tacoma City*, which broke her back and went down in two portions, and the 4,891-ton grain ship *Ullapool*, which settled in mid-channel several hundred yards off the Pier Head, where she remained a prominent landmark. Part of the *Tacoma City's* cargo of steel was retrieved, but the *Ullapool's* was a total loss and, for reasons described later, her hulk was to remain a thorn in the Dock Board's side for a long time to come. The March raids caused 578 deaths and 632 serious injuries, the majority of them in Birkenhead and Wallasey.

April proved to be something of an anticlimax. Only three raids were delivered, killing forty-four and injuring another 125, but with the exception of the tanker *Perso*, damaged in the East Float, no target of importance was hit. On 14 April, while returning from a raid, an He 111 of KG 28 flew into low cloud and crashed in the hills above Aber Falls. The three survivors, one of them injured, made their way down to a house named

Cydgoed, the home of a Mr and Mrs Baxter, who sent for the police. Two of the Germans were young, frightened, glad to be alive and grateful for the tea they were given; the third, evidently a holder of the Knights Cross, remained arrogantly hostile and declined any kindness. It was about par for the course as far as German prisoners were concerned.

Deep within the Fortress, Admiral Noble, who shared his opponent Raeder's views, was puzzled as to why the Luftwaffe was playing cat-and-mouse with the port. 'I often wonder,' he mused, 'why the Germans don't bomb Liverpool for a week on end.'

They were just about to.

17. Another German air-reconnaisance photograph showing Cammell Laird's shipyard at Birkenhead. The basin and graving docks contain warships of every type as well as merchant vessels.

18. Built by Cammell Laird in 1942, the submarine *Saracen* heads down-river to begin her active career

19. Admiral Sir Max Horton, Commander-in-Chief Western Approaches

20. Holidays at Home. A camel welcomes day-trippers on New Brighton landing stage.

21. Captain F.J. Walker, RN, snatches a sandwich during a series of actions in which his Second Support Group sank six U-boats.

22. The Second Support Group, led by Walker in HMS *Starling,* receives a tumultuous welcome on its return to Liverpool.

23. The hospital ship *Atlantis* with 800 sick and wounded men repatriated from German prisoner-of-war camps, berths at the landing stage watched by British and American officers.

4

Holding the Line

Against the background of continuing preparations for Operation Barbarossa, the invasion of the Soviet Union, Adolf Hitler issued his Directive No. 23, *Directions for Operations against the English War Economy,* on 6 February 1941. In it he stressed the importance of destroying the major import harbours, particularly port installations and ships lying or being built in them, following which the smaller harbours would be attacked. While the Wehrmacht was regrouping for Barbarossa, efforts would be intensified not only to inflict the heaviest possible damage, but also to create an impression that the British Isles were themselves to be threatened with invasion again. When attacks against ports were successful, they would be repeated again and again; similarly, the sinking of merchantmen was considered to be of greater importance than that of warships. The overall result of this strategy would be to reduce the United Kingdom's capacity to wage war in Europe and Africa while the invasion of Russia was in progress. Also included in the directive was the perceptive comment that 'No *decisive* success can be expected from terror attacks on residential areas.'

In the meantime, however, things were going very badly indeed for Hitler's ally, Benito Mussolini. The previous October an Italian invasion of Greece had ended in fiasco. In November the Fleet Air Arm had crippled the Italian battle fleet in its base at Taranto. In December the heavily outnumbered British troops in Egypt commenced an offensive which, on the day after Hitler signed his Directive No. 23, culminated in the surrender of the Italian Tenth Army at Beda Fomm. Luftwaffe assistance was promptly despatched to the Mediterranean to restore the situation. Further Luftwaffe units were redeployed to the Balkans for the conquest of Greece and Yugoslavia, which Hitler regarded as being essential for the security of his southern flank during the invasion of Russia. The effect of this was that, in the spring of 1941, the Luftwaffe's strength in Western Europe began to fall dramatically. By the end of April 150 bombers had already been transferred to the Balkans. In May the whole of Luftflotte 2 and all but four groups of Luftflotte 3 were due to follow them east. Thus, while Greece and Yugoslavia were overrun with customary German speed and efficiency and it became possible to set 22 June as the date upon which Barbarossa would commence, the opportunity to inflict a really crippling blow on Liverpool, as Raeder had suggested and Directive No. 23 demanded, was dwindling day by day. At length even Goering accepted that time was running out and Sperrle was ordered to mount a series of *Grossangriffen* against the port throughout the first week of May.

The raid delivered on 1 May was comparatively light. Between 1050 and 0100 hours forty-three bombers dropped forty-eight tons of high explosive and 112 incendiary canisters, each containing thirty-six submunitions, causing damage, loss of life and widespread fires, but the attack was no different from others that had gone before.

On the night of 2 May the raid was somewhat heavier, involving 65 aircraft, and lasted from 2245 until approximately 0245. In Bootle, 200 people were rendered homeless and the city centre sustained further damage. The Dock Board and White Star Buildings were again set on fire, and Church House, the administrative office of the diocese of Liverpool, was gutted. The Liverpool Corn Exchange was competely destroyed, leaving brokers and merchants to conduct their business in the street until alternative premises could be found. During the May Blitz and its immediate aftermath, more business was transacted in coffee houses than at any time since the eighteenth century, leaving the detailed paperwork to follow when it could.

The night of 3/4 May was, without the slightest doubt, the worst in the city's entire history. Luftflotte 3 made a maximum effort and calculated that between 2300 and 0330 no less than 298 bombers had passed over the target area. This was not quite accurate, since a number of aircraft are known to have released their bombs over the Starfish site in the Dee; nor was it a record, since 324 aircraft had been involved in the attack on Merseyside on 26 August and 299 in that on 21 December. The Germans also claimed that 363 tons of high explosive bombs and 1,380 incendiary canisters were dropped, although, for the reason stated above, not all of these found their way into the target. What made the raid such a success for the enemy was that accurate marking by the pathfinder aircraft of KG 26 was followed by equally accurate bombing into the fires already started, which were concentrated within a comparatively small area.

Liverpool was badly hurt. Several hundred fires raged simultaneously across the city and in neighbouring Bootle. In some areas the situation was out of control because water mains had been ruptured by high explosive bombs. From all over the North and Midlands fire brigades converged on Merseyside - some came from as far afield as Scunthorpe, York, Wakefield, West Hartlepool, Derby, Doncaster, Huddersfield and Leicester, and with their assistance the inferno was gradually contained. Had the wind been even stronger than it was that night, it is possible that Liverpool would have sustained the fearful effects of a firestorm, the self-generating phenomenon in which air above a major conflagration rises, sucking in cooler air which soon becomes a fierce wind, fanning the flames to even greater intensity, so that ultimately the searing heat kills everyone within the area. In raids on Hamburg, Dresden and Tokyo, thousands were to die horribly in firestorms which, in the short term, killed more people than the atomic bombs dropped on Hiroshima and Nagasaki. Just how slender was the margin which saved Liverpool from this type of inferno will never be known.

Much of the damage was caused by spreading fires. Almost all of the buildings within the area embraced by the south side of Lord Street, Paradise Street, Canning Place and South Castle Street were either destroyed outright or so severely damaged as to warrant instant demolition. Among the city's superb range of public buildings in William Brown Street the Museum was completely wrecked, part of the Central Library complex was burned out, over 150,000 books being lost in the fire, and the Walker Art Gallery was damaged. In Victoria Street the General Post office sustained heavy damage for the second time and was temporarily forced to transfer its business to the nearby Fruit Exchange; simultaneously, the Bank and Central telephone exchanges were destroyed. India Buildings in Water Street was the seat of numerous small fires but was saved from destruction; not so the Cook Street Arcade, containing the Law Society's library, which was burned out. Lewis's department store in Ranelagh Street was turned into a gutted, calcined shell within which the tenants of the much-loved pets' corner perished horribly. When the fire spread to the nearby Blackler's Stores nothing could be done to save the building because the water mains had been fractured. Off Church Street the Bluecoat School, an eighteenth-century architectural treasure, was seriously damaged by fire but remained standing.

In Bootle a high-explosive bomb struck the Rest Centre in St Andrew's Hall, killing the entire team of twelve WVS workers and forty people who had just lost their homes. The Town Hall was hit and numerous industrial premises were severely damaged, including several timber yards, the gas works, a dye works, a cold storage depot, and a bakery.

Yet, if it was a night of horror, it was a night of heroism too. A heavy bomb exploded in the courtyard at the rear of Mill Road Infirmary, wrecking three buildings and causing serious damage to the rest of the hospital. Many of the ambulances and other vehicles parked in the courtyard caught fire, hindering the rescuers, but somehow 380 patients were got out and transported to other hospitals. One who recovered knowing nothing of his ordeal had been on the operating table when the bomb exploded; his survival was little short of a miracle, since the surgeon and most of his team were killed outright. The evacuation was supervised by the Infirmary's Medical Superintendant, Dr Leonard Findlay, and its Matron, Miss Gertrude Riding, both of whom were already injured; later, their gallantry was recognized by the award, respectively, of the George Medal and the Order of the British Empire. The Mill Road Infirmary incident cost the lives of seventeen members of the medical staff, fifteen ambulance drivers and thirty patients, plus seventy more badly injured.

At the LMS goods yard at Clubmoor, the hour also produced the men, the details being recorded in the December 1941 issue of the railway company's house magazine, *Carry On*.

> During the height of the raid, a munitions train in a siding received a direct hit from a high explosive bomb. For several hours, ten Liverpool men, led by Goods Guard George Roberts, worked at the risk of their lives. Regardless of danger from continuous explosions in the munitions train and from high-explosive bombs which continued to fall in the vicinity, Roberts and his mates strove to minimize the danger and restrict the damage.
>
> Goods Guard Roberts, with Goods Guard Peter Kilshaw and Shunter Evans, were first to go into action. Wagons were ablaze from the explosion and Roberts quickly realised that unless something was done, the fire would spread. He and his colleagues started to uncouple wagons immediately in front of those that were burning. While they strove, other help was on the way. Driver Robert

Bate and Fireman George Wilkinson, together with Goods Guard James Edward Rowland were on duty in a nearby siding. Immediately they volunteered to proceed to the scene and succeeded in drawing wagons in adjacent sidings away from danger. Driver Alexander Ritchie and Fireman William Frederick Fowler also volunteered to take a light engine to the scene and they assisted in drawing wagons onto roads away from the actual fire. Goods Guard John Guinan assisted in the work of uncoupling wagons so that they might be drawn away to safety.

Before the first engines on the scene could get to work, the drivers had to be given the road; and here Goods Guard Kilshaw came into action again. With considerable initiative he obtained access to the yard box, which was closed, and after studying the diagram, set the road for the engine to run into the sidings. Later, after he had returned to his depot, Kilshaw volunteered to work the fire train to the sidings and again opened the levers in the box.

For the final phase of this night's heroic story, we must go to Signalman Peter William Stringer. When the bomb fell on the munitions train, Stringer was standing at the top of the steps of his box, keeping a lookout for incendiaries. The force of the explosion threw him down the steps and to the bottom of an embankment. Despite injury to his leg, and the severe shaking he had received, Stringer, realising the possible danger to traffic, endeavoured to get in touch with control, but the box telephone had been rendered useless. Next he tried a public call box, outside the station, but that was dead too. Not to be beaten, Stringer set off down the road to the nearest fire station, but fortunately meeting an ARP cyclist messenger, sent him off with the message. Next Stringer got in touch with the ARP wardens, and advised them to get people in surrounding houses into shelter. He then made his way to the next signalbox and advised the signalman there to stop all traffic. Stringer then returned to his own signalbox.

If anything, the professionalism of the account understates the case. Exploding ammunition and falling bombs had wrecked houses in the surrounding streets, and among those severely damaged was that of Lewis and Kit Rider in Missouri Road. The Riders were typical of many young couples of the time in that they had had a long courtship, lasting over six years, before they had married, and during this they had collected enough to furnish their home, into which they had moved shortly before the outbreak of war. Lew was a stonemason and when their Anderson shelter had been issued he had made a splendid job of erecting it in the back garden. The entrance faced away from the house, so that falling rubble would not block it, and was further protected by a blast wall. He had dug deep, laid a concrete base over which he had built a wooden floor, reinforced the headcover with large stones from a neighbouring field, run an electric cable from the house and painted the interior white. There was room for a double mattress and a crib for their baby daughter and all was made as snug and safe as it could possibly be.

In December 1940 Lew enlisted voluntarily and joined the Royal Engineers. Kit, knowing that neighbours across the road did not have their own shelter, allowed them to use hers while she and the baby went to the Anderson next door. The entrance to this faced the house and the shelter itself had not been so well dug in, so that whenever a bomb exploded nearby the whole structure heaved. During this incident the rear of the houses collapsed, burying the shelter. Kit, the baby and the other occupants were not dug out until 11.00 next morning; Kit's own shelter was unharmed.

Lew, stationed at Blacon, near Chester, managed to get home and a day or so later he and Kit returned to salvage what they could of their belongings. He was particularly anxious to recover his mason's tools from a shelf in the coalhouse, and, amidst the general devastation, paid little attention to a hole in the roof of the building. Suddenly he noticed something unusual protruding from the neatly piled coal.

'What's this thing with the hook on?' he called.

The thing with the hook on was a 500-kilo unexploded

bomb, which required the prompt attention of the nearest bomb disposal team.

Kit never told him that she had not been using the shelter on which he had laboured so hard, but she and the baby were evacuated to the peace and quiet of Mynydd Llandegai, near Bangor, where she spent the next two years.

Fires were also raging from one end of the docks to the other. Lying in Huskisson Dock's No. 2 Branch was the Brocklebank Line's 7,649-ton freighter *Malakand* with 1,000 tons of high-explosive bombs aboard destined for the Middle East. Shortly after the raid started a drifting and partly deflated barrage balloon settled on the forward deck of the vessel and soon began to blaze fiercely, possibly ignited by an incendiary bomb. Under the direction of the ship's master, Captain Howard Cooke Kinley, the crew manned their pumps and brought the situation under control within fifteen minutes, despite the arrival aboard of several more incendiaries.

However, the nearby dock sheds had been struck by high-explosive bombs. Uncontrollable fires started and threatened to engulf the ship. Ordering his crew ashore, Kinley made his way through the inferno to the auxiliary fire station at North West Huskisson No. 1, only to find it deserted. The fire crews were already heavily engaged in nearby dock sheds and Kinley found them there, explaining the position to John Lappin, the senior officer present. Lappin immediately telephoned for reinforcements and then directed his own few men and the *Malakand's* crew in a desperate fight to save the ship, despite the terrible danger involved. By 0300 the fire had taken a firm hold on *Malakand* and the situation had become critical. Lappin rang the Chief Fire Officer who agreed to despatch a tender with oxyacetylene cutting equipment so that a hole could be cut in the port side of the hull with a view to scuttling the ship. This duly arrived, but before anything could be done the major part of the deadly cargo exploded with a thunderous roar. The immediate area of the dock was blown flat; one of the ship's four-ton anchors flew 100 yards to crash into the engines of a Dock Board hopper; steel plates were hurled a distance of 2½ miles; and the blast wrecked the nearest Overhead Railway station as well as seriously damaging a section of the elevated track. Kinley and several men were injured yet, incredibly, only four people were killed, two of them in a car on the Dock Road which was crushed by a section of plating. Smaller explosions continued to convulse the tortured hulk of the *Malakand* until the fire burned itself out three days later.

Far above the city, the Defiant night fighters of 96 Squadron, flying from Cranage, could see the inferno raging below. The enemy bombers were silhouetted against the fires as they crossed the target area in waves, with anti-aircraft shells bursting among them. The Defiants banked steeply and dived at them, machine guns blazing from their turrets. Luftflotte 3 lost a higher proportion of aircraft that night than in any other major attack on Liverpool, but its casualties remained well within acceptable limits; most serious was the loss of three of KG 26's He 111s, the wreckage of which revealed the secrets of the *Y-Geraet*.

Another view of the embattled city was recorded for posterity by the artist Grainger Smith from his home in Wallasey. The flames, reflected in the river, reach hundreds of feet into the air beneath a lowering blanket of smoke. In the background, beyond the dark outline of the famous waterfront, the skeletons of burning buildings resemble broken teeth and the rose-red sandstone of the Cathedral throws back the reflection of the fires.

Our own view was less dramatic. When the All Clear sounded we emerged from the cellar and stood on the steps of the house, looking up Edge Lane towards the ridge beneath which lay the city centre. Suddenly, it all seemed very quiet. The sky was red, tinged with flickering orange. The air was acrid with the smell of burning. Fragments of ash and blackened scraps of paper were drifting down. Something heavier was smouldering in the privet hedge; it was a small square of blanket, charred around the edges.

Sunday 4 May was anything but a day of rest. Firemen from forty brigades battled to bring the fires under control while a 6,000-strong army of labourers, including 2,680 soldiers detailed for the task, set to under the direction of the City Building Surveyor, clearing the roads and demolishing the most dangerous buildings. For the sake of speed, many buildings were brought down with explosive charges laid by the Royal Engineers or shot-firers brought in from the nearest coalfields. Picks and shovels were augmented by every mechanical excavator and digger that could be brought into service, and hundreds of lorries were requisitioned.

Among those toiling like ants were two groups of men in unfamiliar uniforms, manning huge mechanical excavators. The latter had just arrived from the United States under the terms of the Lend-Lease Agreement and were accompanied by a detachment of the US Army Engineer Corps which was to instruct Royal Engineer personnel in their use. These were the first American troops to be seen in Liverpool since World War I, when large numbers had passed through the port and had been temporarily billeted in a purpose-built transit camp at Knotty Ash. Even the privates, many of whom were coloured, smoked expensive-looking cigars, and they were all cheerily informal, hailing senior service officers and municipal officials alike as 'Buddy' or 'Mac'. Nobody minded in the least. The seriousness of the situation had led to the Americans' commanding officer being requested to release the machines and, although the United States was still technically neutral, he had done better than that by sending his boys along as well. They worked with a will, cascading huge loads of rubble into the waiting lorries with an enthusiasm that threatened to shatter the vehicles.

For the moment, the millions of tons of rubble were simply piled on their original sites, leaving the roadways clear, but were later transported to specially established tips. Some of the clearance work had an unreal, even weird, yet entirely logical character. In one of the principal shopping streets, for example, crowds of resting soldiers, provided with bottles of beer by a thoughtful well-wisher, lounged on expensive three-piece suites rescued from a furniture store while, nearby, firemen damped down the previous night's fires. Regarding the scene, Tom Griffiths, by day the proprietor of the Bedford Stores in Bedford Street and by night an AFS fireman, suddenly found himself laughing; like others, wearied by the terrible night's work, he felt that the alternative was to go mad.

Simultaneously, work was in hand to restore the more important gas, water and electricity supplies and to re-establish vital telephone links. Journalists arriving at the Victoria Street offices of the *Liverpool Daily Post* to work on Monday morning's edition found the building without gas, water, electricity, telephone or telegraphic connections. Since the appearance of the paper was considered essential to maintaining morale, restoring power for the presses was given priority by the authorities and, shortly before the deadline, a mains cable connection was effected; this, together with the paper's standby diesel generators, proved sufficient. Details of news outside the city was generously provided by the *Manchester Guardian* and *Evening News* for a period of several weeks until normal communications were restored, a regular shuttle of cars being established between Liverpool and Manchester.

As Sunday wore on, there was a general and quite spontaneous movement into the city centre, and we joined it. People, sensing that history was being made, simply wished to see for themselves. There were piles of bricks and masonry everywhere, with girders and beams protruding from them. There were tramlines twisted into impossible shapes, leaning lamp standards and trailing overhead power cables. Feet crunched on billions of broken glass splinters which sparkled in the evening sunlight. Everywhere, one stepped over emergency water mains, laid above ground for the sake of speed; these sometimes crossed the road and, where they did, ramps were being constructed for motor vehicles to pass over them, although they barred the passage of trams for some time to come. At every corner familiar landmarks had vanished or been reduced to gutted shells. Like many others, my grandfather had come to Liverpool in the 1880s, when the streets were paved with gold, and he had worked hard and prospered; he loved the city and, in common with those around us, the sights moved him to tears of rage and sadness. Yet, if that visit to the city centre allowed people to express their anger, and even reinforced the will to win, the crowds got in the way of those with vital work to complete. They said as much, and so did the police, and so did no less a person than the Lord Mayor; so we went home.

At midnight the Luftwaffe returned, but by the standards of the previous night the raid was trivial, involving only fifty aircraft in a low-intensity attack which petered out around 0400. The only building of note to be destroyed was the Rotunda Theatre in Scotland Road, where many famous variety names had played. In the river the 6,770-ton *Silver Sandal,* with a deck cargo of aircraft, was holed by a high-explosive bomb and set on fire by incendiaries. With the assistance of a fireboat the blaze was extinguished and she was towed into Birkenhead, where her aircraft were unloaded.

Monday was, of course, a working day, but movement of traffic within the city had been made extremely difficult by the cumulative damage sustained during the weekend, although clearance work was continuing. The Dock Road was blocked in eight places and access to the northern docks was temporarily denied because of the destruction of bridges over the Liverpool and Leeds Canal. Dale Street remained open but quickly became congested with horsedrawn wagons, which were still employed in large numbers by local carriers. To give the clearance teams every opportunity to complete their work, it was decided that only essential traffic should be allowed into the city. Two cordons were set up by the police, the outer along the line of Queen's Drive, between three and four miles from the city centre and the inner along the line of the old boundary, two miles from the centre. At these, vehicles approaching the city were stopped and unless their drivers carried a pass or could convince the officers that their business was vital, they were turned back. Trams continued to run on routes where the permanent way was undamaged, a mere thirteen per cent of the whole, and buses were brought in from neighbouring boroughs to make good the shortfall.

That morning, the senior management of the railways met to discuss the damage inflicted on the local system. Except at Langton Dock, all lines leading into the docklands goods stations were blocked by craters, piles of rubble or unexploded bombs. Lack of water for fire fighting meant that a fire was still burning in Exchange Station. The viaduct running north from the station had sustained further damage and although restoration work was in hand trains running inwards from Southport, Ormskirk and Wigan were terminating respectively at Seaforth, Walton Junction and Preston Road, where arrangements had been made to ferry passengers into the city by bus. Some 300 yards of the Edge Hill to Bootle branch line had been destroyed near Breck Road, but 200 infantrymen of the North and South Staffordshire Regiments had been made available and, with their assistance, it was anticipated that the track would be repaired in a fortnight's time, restoring communication with Canada and Alexandra Docks. The arrival sidings at Aintree goods yard were working but ten departure roads were blocked. At Kirkdale Station the entrance and steps leading down to the platform had been destroyed. There were unexploded bombs at Marsh Lane Junction, in the cutting at Fontenoy Street and behind Fazakerley West signal box. The line to Riverside Station had been cut. After due consideration of these and many similar matters it was decided that the following should have priority: disposal of the bomb at Marsh Lane Junction and clearance of the route between Aintree and Atlantic Junction; restoration of the viaduct between Sandhills and Exchange Stations; clearance of the departure roads at Aintree; provision of stairs at Kirkdale Station; restoration of the Edge Hill - Bootle and Waterloo Dock branch lines.

Incredibly, the huge marshalling yard at Edge Hill was barely touched. When, as I often did, I went to watch the shunting that afternoon, it was working as normally as ever. The adjacent Botanic Gardens and the park surrounding them, however, contained hundreds of small pits left by incendiaries and a stick of high-explosive bombs had gouged a crater in the bank of an ornamental lake, wrecked an aviary and shattered the greenhouse. The bomb-aimers had been fractionally out in their calculations. Nevertheless, during the week the volume of traffic handled by the Liverpool railway system had been reduced by forty-seven per cent.

Everyone was now beginning to feel the effects of lost sleep, but at at 0020 the Alert began wailing for the fifth night in succession. The raid lasted until 0415 and, while not intense, was accurate and started widespread fires. The Cathedral had a narrow escape when a bomb changed direction after penetrating the roof of the south transept, smashing through an outer wall to explode above the street; even so, a huge area of stained glass was shattered and incendiaries started a fire in the contractor's yard at the uncompleted west end of the building. St Luke's Church at the top of Bold Street, the most beautiful in the city centre, was completely gutted by fire; its shell and tower, still pleasing to the eye, now lie surrounded by quiet gardens, preserved as a memorial to those people of Liverpool who gave their lives during the attack on the city. In the Town Hall, the council chamber was so badly damaged that meetings had to be held in the municipal annexe, along Dale Street; scars left by this bomb can still be traced in the wall of the old Liverpool and London Globe Insurance Company's building across High Street.

Once again, the Fire Brigade was stretched to the limit, with the result that heavy responsibilities were thrust on the junior ranks, witness the report of Fire Constable Thomas Jones on the events of the night:

> At 0200 hours of Tuesday 6 May 1941 I was instructed by Chief Inspector Williams to take charge of No. 17 Pump, Constable 249H and a crew from Lytham St Annes and

proceed to the new Royal [Telephone] Exchange, Colquitt Street. I arrived on the scene at 0205 hours and found part of the old school used by the GPO and attached to the exchange, on fire and spreading rapidly to the new building. I was unable to obtain water from the street mains and proceeded to Cornwallis Street Baths with the object of pumping from same, but discovered that they had been emptied. I despatched a message to the Central Fire Station informing them of what had occurred and that I was proceeding to the docks for the purpose of obtaining water. We eventually coupled up with three lengths of suction hose into the Salthouse Dock and with the assistance of pumps B6145, FYY 158 and crews, brought one branch to bear onto the school used by the GPO and situated next to the exchange. I passed word 'Fire Under' at 0250 hours and then concentrated on other fires which were raging in the vicinity. At about this time, two more pumps, B3632 with a crew from Wolverhampton and C1139 with a crew from Hinckley, arrived and with the help of hose buses from Shaw Street, Simpson Street and Edge Lane we managed to maintain four deliveries from No. 17 Pump to relay pumps working in pairs and tackled all the fires in this district. These fires were eventually brought under control at about 0900 hours, Tuesday May 6th. The following is a list of premises which we dealt with between the hours of 0200 and 1130, Tuesday 6th.

1. New Royal (Telephone) Exchange, Colquitt Street. St Luke's School. East wing destroyed.
2. 23, 25 and 27 Seel Street. Technical College of Domestic Science and City Technical School for Women. Damage considerable.
3. Buildings between 64 and 82 Duke Street. Completely destroyed. Concentrated on property adjoining, viz. 64 Duke Street, Liverpool Magneto Service and Repairs, 82 84 Duke Street, Peter Walker & Son Ltd.
4. 43 Duke Street. Legge House. Roof partly destroyed.
5. 3 storey building and entrance to factory, Parr Street and Wolstenholme Square. Occupiers, McEaden and Company, cork manufacturers; Hughes and Treleaven, printer's ink manufacturers (works); City Shoe Repair Company; Jas. Gittins, tea dealer; W. Crosland and

> Company, manufacturing stationers; E.A. Busher, printers; E. Dyson, lithographers; John Hall and Company. 3 storey building fronting Duke Street, damage trifling; factory at rear, fronting Wolstenholme Square and Parr Street, destroyed.

Jones had displayed cool courage, exemplary initiative and outstanding leadership while the world blazed and crashed about his ears. Nevertheless, as a regular he was conscious that he had not fully discharged his duties and he apologized for the fact in the final paragraph of his report, completed on 14 May:

'Owing to circumstances, time, etc, I have been unable to obtain the names and addresses of the owners of the premises involved.' No such apology was required and the following day he was commended by the Chief Officer. It is pleasing, but not surprising, to note that he later entered the senior ranks of his service.

Nevertheless, still more was demanded of Liverpool and its people as the ordeal continued. A raid of similar intensity, duration and accuracy was delivered during the night of 6/7 May, undoing much of the repair work which had been done. Brunswick and Harrington Docks sustained further damage and Princes Landing Stage was hit. Bent's Brewery was the seat of a serious fire, as was Cooper's Building in Church Street, famous for the smell of roasting coffee which always seemed to surround it. Bombs also fell in the central business area.

Sperrle now decided to administer what he hoped would be the *coup de grâce*. On the night of 7/8 May Luftflotte 3 made a maximum effort and 166 bombers droned over the target area in waves, starting at 0030. When the raid ended approximately four hours later, they had dropped 232 tons of high-explosive bombs and 807 incendiary canisters. The raiders had, however, lost some of their previous accuracy, and their bomb loads were scattered across Liverpool, Bootle and Wallasey. Even so, over 300 incidents were reported and fires raged over a wide area. The defenders, now deadly tired, were further hampered by the debris of a week's continuous night attacks which hindered the movement of fire engines, ambulances and rescue vehicles.

Tragically, the brunt of the damage sustained in this raid was borne by private houses, particularly in Bootle, where entire streets were flattened.

Seven nights' battering had reduced the dock system to a shambles of gutted sheds, rubble-strewn quays and smashed hydraulic machinery, choked with sunken and severely damaged shipping. Sir Lionel Warner, the Dock Board's General Manager, a strong man of wide experience and shrewd judgement who had joined the organization from the London and North Western Railway in 1914, did not mince his words when he described the situation which existed on the morning of 8 May.

> The whole way from Gladstone to Sandon, inclusive, there are no [river] entrances working and no power. The Brocklebank Dock is blocked off entirely for the time being and the ships in there are locked in. The Overhead Railway is down in several places. If we can get the obstruction at Canada removed we shall be able to work our dock [railway] line through from Gladstone as far as Canning. We are very helpless in the meantime as there are no railway [goods] stations open to receive dockhauled traffic although some are receiving carted traffic.

Not even the Dock Board's normally specific records reveal the precise date of the marine casualties, since many vessels were hit more than once. In Gladstone Dock the tug *Bison* had gone down. In Alexandra Dock the freighter *Roxburgh Castle,* with general cargo aboard, had sunk, and so had five smaller vessels, including two derrick barges, a flat and two elevator barges. In Canada Dock the coaster *Domino* lay capsized and the 6,589-ton *Elstree Grange* had burned to the water line; neither would sail again. Nor would the freighter *Bra Kar,* now a gutted hulk, nor several flats and a derrick barge, burned out and sunk. *Baron Inchcape,* with grain and cattle cake in her holds, was down by the head as a result of direct hits; nearby, the 7,924-ton *Tacoma Star,* similarly wounded, rested on the bottom. In Langton Dock four vessels had been sunk: the floating crane *Hercules,* the dredger *Stylus,* the tug *Hornby* and the freighter *Trentino.* A second freighter, the 4,969-ton *Marton,* was burned out in Langton Graving Dock. In Huskisson Dock ammunition experts were sifting through the still-warm skeleton of the *Malakand,* and the coaster *Stromboli* lay semi-submerged on her side after receiving a direct hit in the engine room; also littering the bed of the dock were the wrecks of a steam hopper and several flats. In Albert Dock the bows had been blown off the lightship *Sirius* and she had sunk at once. In Brocklebank Graving Dock the liner *Europa,* still being repaired after the damage she had sustained the previous December, was again hit and sank after burning herself out. In King's Dock near misses damaged the freighters *Clan MacInnes* and *Mimosa,* but they were kept afloat with salvage pumps. Direct hits sank the tug *Bonita* and a hopper in Waterloo dock, and another tug, *Enid Blanche,* was sunk by a near miss in the East Brocklebank Branch. In Salthouse and Stanley docks several coal barges were hit and sunk.

Nor did the Mersey ferries escape. *Claughton* was temporarily put out of commission when a bomb, fortunately of small calibre, wrecked her saloon while she was in mid-passage, and *Bidston's* upperworks were battered by flying blocks of masonry while she was lying at the Landing Stage. The saddest loss of all was *Royal Daffodil II,* sunk at her moorings at Seacombe Stage during the early hours of 8 May when a near miss stove in her hull. She was probably the most popular ship on the river and, like her sister, *Royal Iris II,* had inherited the distinctive honorific earned by their predecessors, *Daffodil* and *Iris,* when they covered themselves with glorv at Zeebrugge on St George's Day, 1918. In the interests of morale, salvage work on her began at the earliest possible moment.

On the night of 8 May people went to bed fully expecting to be woken as usual by the sirens, but there was only blessed silence. It was the same the next night and the one after and soon it was clear that the Luftwaffe had ended its offensive against the city. Liverpool had taken a fearful beating, becoming the most heavily bombed target in the United Kingdom outside London and, towards the end of this horrendous week it seemed that the city of the merchant princes might be dying. In Liverpool itself this series of seven raids killed 1,453 and seriously injured 1,065; in Bootle, the figures were 257 killed and twenty-six seriously injured; in Birkenhead twenty-eight killed and forty-four seriously injured; in Wallasey, three killed and nineteen seriously injured. Much of the city lay in ruins, and most of the docks were clogged with wreckage. 'I shudder to think what would have happened if the blitz had gone on for three more days,' commented Admiral Noble. Another three days would certainly have put the port out of action for months to come; in purely analytical terms, another ten days would have destroyed its capacity altogether, with incalculable results.

During this series of raids, and indeed those which had gone before, the abnormal became normal to the point that incidents which would otherwise have been discarded by fiction writers as too improbable actually became fact. There was, for example, the story of Fire Sergeant Roy Fletcher, who disappeared without trace while fighting fires in Forth Street during the terrible night of 3 May. Unrecognizable human remains were subsequently found and he was reported missing, presumed killed. Seventeen days later he was found alive but injured and suffering from loss of memory in Warrington Infirmary, twenty miles distant. How he had got there, and what had happened to him in the meantime, remained a mystery.

Many incidents served to emphasize the collective lunacy of the situation. On hearing the air raid siren, a middle-aged couple had scrambled from their bed, pausing only to collect their false teeth from the bedside glass, and had headed quickly for the nearest public shelter. What followed was the most painful time of their lives, as they had each inserted the wrong teeth and were too embarrassed to effect the exchange in front of strangers. One man, found scrabbling furiously in the debris of a large crater, was asked what he was doing and replied that he was looking for his new hat, which had been blown off by the explosion. For the moment, the loss of his pride and joy obscured the fact that he had escaped death by a whisker. Another, on the point of entering his house, was suddenly blown into the road, where he lay unconscious for a while. When he came to, he found that he was still clutching the door knob; the door itself lay buried under the wreckage of the building.

Some of the best stories came from the rescue teams. One team, startled by shrill shouts of 'Hello there!' from beneath the ruins of a house already reported clear by the ARP Warden, began digging at once. It was assumed that the victim was probably deaf, because every attempt to reassure him that help was on the way was met with further shouts of 'Hello there!' At length the men broke through to an air pocket containing a parrot in a battered cage; the bird, shocked into silence by the destruction of his home, was now in full voice. In another incident, a team were passing the heaped rubble of buildings from which they had effected several rescues three days earlier when they heard what they took to be the mewing of a kitten. Despite their fatigue they dug down and at length uncovered a week-old baby.

Perhaps best of all was the story of the elderly lady, buried when her house collapsed on top of her Morrison shelter. The rescue team worked their way towards her and eventually established contact.

'You OK in there, love?'

'Yes, thanks. I'm all right.'

'Don't worry, now - there's a big strong lad on his way in to help you!'

The response was a dry chuckle.

'A big strong lad's no use to me at my time of life! Can't you send a nice old feller with pots of money?'

Sometimes, the question arises as to whether civilian morale had begun to crack towards the end of that week. Certainly, there were dangerous fools about, always willing to exaggerate the worst aspects of any situation, but such people can be found everywhere. Among the weak-minded and credulous there were rumours of a death toll well in excess of 20,000; of trains leaving the city, packed with bodies for secret cremation; of food riots; of peace demonstrations; of martial law being imposed. None of this had the slightest foundation in fact, nor was it generally believed. A more balanced picture was drawn by General Pile.

> There can be no doubt at all that if the series of raids had been continued, Merseyside would have been useless for a long while. The strain on all branches of the defence, military and civil, was enormous. In addition, in Liverpool civilian morale had touched a lower level by the last night of the raids than at any other time in any other place during the Blitz, and I am not surprised. I spent two nights in Liverpool at this time, and it was most unpleasant. But, at low level or not, morale held. No one, however old or however young, is out of the firing line, and, while the soldiers and airmen may destroy enemy raiders, it is the citizens themselves who are the last line of defence. If they give way, if they do not restore immediately what has been destroyed, if they fail to get the wounded away to hospital, if they do not get the normal services of the city working again, then a blockade will, sooner or later, be successful. It is greatly to the credit of Merseyside that, in spite of an attack more severe in its weight, its concentration, and its continuity than that experienced by any other provincial centre, the port remained in action to receive the supplies that were flooding in from the United States.

On balance, it is probable that General Pile's view of morale erred on the side of pessimism and may have been influenced by the fact that, from the night of Sunday 4 May onwards, people began leaving the city in large numbers every evening. The great majority came from the docklands neighbourhoods which were directly in the target area. They made their way to Formby, Maghull and Ormskirk, where they were allowed to sleep in barns, church halls and cinemas, and to the woods at Huyton, where they camped out. All they wanted was a night's undisturbed rest in relative safety. In the morning, they returned to the city and got on with their jobs. The idea won official approval since it solved several problems for the authorities. For the people to remain in the areas most exposed to enemy action was simply to invite further casualties, yet it was wrong to order them to abandon their homes. It was better for all concerned that they should leave of their own accord with controlled assistance, since this would relieve the strain on the rescue services and the dwindling number of Rest Centres remaining in operation, while simultaneously permitting the repair and clearance teams to continue with their work unhindered. Tickets were issued which enabled those who wanted to leave to use either the railway or convoys of army lorries assembled for the purpose. During the last night of the attack about 50,000 people left the city under this scheme. One account speaks of people forming orderly queues with their belongings, laughing and joking among themselves, always with a cheer for the convoys of extra police and troops drafted into the area to assist. This does not sound like demoralization.

If those sleeping under the trees at Huyton, some with relatives to bury, others with homes in ruins, all of them deadly tired and uncertain what the morrow might bring, had been told they had just won a stunning victory, they could not have believed it. There were no visible grounds at all for such an apparently absurd claim, yet, in the long term, it was a fact.

5

Soldiering On

Liverpool's ordeal during the first week of May 1941 receives the briefest of mentions in the official history, possibly because many targets throughout the United Kingdom were hit simultaneously, including Plymouth, Belfast and, of course, London. This dilution of the maximum effort required to destroy a target of critical importance before the bulk of the Luftwaffe was transferred to the East was a major strategic error on Goering's part, compounded by Sperrle at the tactical level. Had the heavy raid on Liverpool during the night of 3/4 May been followed by an equally heavy attack the following night, it is probable that most of the water mains, essential for fire fighting, would have been destroyed, leaving the city terribly vulnerable to subsequent raids. As it was, a series of comparatively light raids was mounted, enabling the repair crews to maintain a water supply that was just adequate. Even so, when a medium-strength raid was delivered on the night of 7/8 May the cumulative effects of the damage became apparent at once. In the light of this, therefore, Sperrle can be seen to have made a second mistake in mounting no further major attacks on the port. On the other hand, he may have felt that he had completed his task, since reconnaissance flights would have revealed much of the city in ruins, the docksides a mass of rubble and twisted metal with 69 out of 144 cargo berths inoperable, the docks themselves littered with 80,000 tons of sunken or damaged shipping and the railway system cut in numerous places. He probably believed that the port was out of action and would remain so for many months; given the impending deadline of Barbarossa, further diversion of his dwindling resources could be regarded as pointless. Nevertheless, Sperrle's assessment of the situation failed to take into account two essential factors. The first was the astonishing resilience, energy and determination of Liverpool's people; the second was the expertise of the Dock Board's engineering and salvage departments.

In fact, the Luftwaffe had not quite finished with Liverpool. Minor raids took place on 29 and 31 May, causing some damage in Gladstone and Alexandra Docks. Inexplicably, on the latter occasion some of the aircraft bound for Liverpool released their bombs over Dublin, killing twenty-eight and seriously injuring eighty-seven. The incident did nothing to foster good relations between Eire and Germany, and, in passing, it is worth mentioning that, despite their neutrality, many Irishmen were already opposed to Prime Minister De Valera's anti-British stance. The proportion of men volunteering for service with the armed forces of the Crown was the same as that in the Dominions and, when Belfast was raided, the Dublin Fire Brigade raced north to help, headlights blazing in blatant disregard of the blackout regulations. German aircrews crash-landing in Eire found themselves interned for the duration of the war; RAF crews in a similar predicament were often helpfully, if unofficially, directed to the border.

After this, only reconnaissance flights, sometimes armed with a few bombs, paid periodic visits to Liverpool. Incursions took place on 25 June, 24 July and 1 November, but did little damage. On 10 January 1942 a stick of four bombs, the last to fall on the city, destroyed a row of houses in Upper Stanhope Street, killing fifteen. Enemy aircraft were reported over Merseyside as late as 9 August 1942, but to all intents and purposes the Luftwaffe had gone. Most of the men who had bombed Liverpool were to find cold graves in the Russian steppeland. In France the strength of Luftflotte 3 was steadily eroded by the demands of other theatres until it was no longer a force to be reckoned with. When the Allies invaded Normandy in June 1944 it was a mere shadow of its former self, quite incapable of offering effective opposition. Sperrle was somewhat unfairly dismissed and was never re-employed. He was acquitted of war crimes at Nuremberg in 1948 and died an embittered man five years later.

All of this lay in the future and in May 1941 the people of Liverpool could only assume that they had been granted a temporary respite as they began to clear the wreckage. First, there were the dead to bury. There were over 1,700 of them, men, women and children, more than could be coped with by the hard-pressed mortuary service. On 13 May the remains of 550 were buried in a brick vault at Anfield Cemetery during a moving service conducted by the city's senior churchmen of every denomination. In the hospitals there were 1,200 seriously injured to be cared for. These figures, however, reflected but a small part of the misery inflicted. There were 51,000 homeless people in Liverpool and another 25,000 in Bootle. Somehow, the billeting service found most of them accommodation in the area but such was the immensity of the problem that almost 10,000 had to be evacuated to towns in Lancashire and Cheshire. Taking previous raids into account, over 10,000 houses had been completely destroyed in Liverpool, Birkenhead, Bootle and Wallasey, while over 184,000 had been damaged; proportionately, Bootle was hardest hit, with fewer than one house in ten remaining intact. Servicemen, granted compassionate leave, found their neighbourhood in ruins and their families and friends scattered across the city. They found, too, that much of the city centre, containing the familiar landmarks of their youth, no longer existed.

The City Council, fully conscious of the immense burden being shouldered by the people and wishing to provide them with some means of escape from their troubles, passed a resolution on 8 May permitting cinemas to open on Sundays. The resolution was not without its opponents, for in Liverpool, the city of contrasts, the unbridled enjoyment of Saturday night was traditionally followed by strict observance of the Sabbath. The circumstances undoubtedly warranted the change and, as the formidable Councillor Mrs Elizabeth Braddock, a powerful figure in Liverpool politics, commented with irrefutable logic during the debate: 'Those who do not want Sunday entertainment can keep away.'

The Herculean task of clearing the wreckage was the responsibility of the Debris Clearance and Road Repair Service, under the control of Mr Herbert Hamer, the City Engineer and Surveyor. His labour force, consisting of 3,000 servicemen, 2,000 men employed by civil engineering contractors from Merseyside and Manchester, and 1,000 otherwise unemployed men sent by the labour exchanges, had already been hard at work during the week of continuous attacks. Its priority was now to reopen the 500 roads, including most of the arterial highways, which had been closed as a direct result of enemy action. Some were blocked by debris, others were unsafe to use because the gutted buildings which bordered them still had to be demolished, and others were closed off because they contained unexploded bombs or ruptured gas and water mains. The principal object was to clear routes for the fire and ambulance services in case the Luftwaffe should return, but in achieving this the clearance teams also restored the city's ability to go about its daily business. Temporary tips were established at Byrom Street, Pitt Street and Netherfield Road, and on these were departed millions of tons of rubble brought by requisitioned lorries. The main roads were cleared quickly, but some of the less important side streets remained blocked for several weeks. The total cost of the operation, including restoration of pavements, was estimated at £250,000. One lesson which had been learned during the first week of May was that there could never be too many sources of water for fire fighting. When many bomb sites were cleared and levelled, therefore, brick-built emergency water supply (EWS) cisterns were built on them; the best known of these was located on the corner of Castle Street and Cook Street, where the surviving arches of the former arcade were reflected on the water in the manner of a Roman bath.

Simultaneously, the water, gas, electricity and telephone authorities were stretched to the limit restoring vital services on the basis of strict priorities. Three of the city's reservoirs, Kensington, Breeze Hill and High Park Street, had been damaged but remained workable. The water mains themselves were fractured or leaking in 700 places and in some cases long lengths of mains pipe had to be relaid. This involved depriving some areas of water for a period, but where this was necessary mobile water tankers, supplemented by milk carts, were employed to provide a domestic supply. Over 500 gas mains were broken, the Liverpool Gas Company's repair teams being joined by those of neighbouring gas companies to restore the service. The power stations of Clarence Dock and Lister Drive had both been hit but remained in operation, although thirty-four electricity sub-stations were out of action and there were over 700 breaks in underground cables. Post Office engineers worked round the clock to restore communication, absolute priority being given to Headquarters Western Approaches. Elsewhere, railwaymen re-established their links with the docks, tramway engineers restrung overhead power cables and repaired damaged track, and workmen laboured to render damaged houses habitable.

The essential services were restored very quickly, although the work would continue for months to come. Yet, every hour of every day of every week, something would be returned to normal. Water would flow from a tap; there was gas to cook with again; there was electric light and one could listen to the radio once more; a telephone would ring; a street would be reopened to traffic; trams were running again on this route or that; a family returned to their repaired home. Shock faded, to be replaced by quiet optimism. And still the Luftwaffe did not return.

The reinforcement fire contingents left for home, as did the numerous buses which had arrived to operate on the routes of the temporarily dislocated tramway system. By 16 May restoration of the latter had progessed sufficiently for the city's Passenger Transport Executive to offer their formal thanks to Manchester, St Helens and Southport Corporation Passenger Transport Departments, Crosville Motor Services Ltd, Ribble Motor Services Ltd and British Insulated Cables Ltd for their help in restoring services affected by enemy action.

As in the city, so in the docks, save that the problems were somewhat more complicated. Here, sunken and damaged vessels apart, the tangle of wreckage resembled a puzzle set by a demonic genius. An outsider would not have known where to begin, but the Dock Board Engineer's Department took the chaos in its stride. Its first priority was the restoration of the hydraulic power upon which the working of dock gates and bridges depended. Fractured water mains and damaged pumping stations had to be repaired as quickly as possible. Destruction of the city's mains had left the Stanley and Canada pumping stations dry and petrol pumps were employed to lift water from the docks into the return tanks until the normal supply could be resumed. Damaged dock gates had to be lifted, removed, repaired and replaced. Many sheds were either gutted or so badly damaged that they were unusable. They were swept away and their sites became open quays, equipped with temporary lighting and mobile cranes. The berth where the *Malakand* had exploded, fortunately one of the oldest and shallowest in the Huskisson system, was simply filled in and used as a cargo-handling space. There were, too, wrecked cranes, damaged railway track and burned-out rolling stock among the mountains of debris At one period over 1,300 men and 162 tipping lorries were employed solely in clearing the rubble, the last of which was not removed until August. Nevertheless, amid the devastation, one gleaming fact emerged - old

Jesse Hartley's immense granite walls, the very heart of the port, had withstood everything the Luftwaffe could do to them. Incredible as it may seem, with the repair work barely begun, dockers were able to work full shifts as early as 9 May.

The salvage of the vessels sunk within the docks, and indeed within the entire operating area covered by the port, was the responsibility of the Dock Board's Marine Department, directed by Captain H.V. Hart, RNR, a fine seaman and master of his craft, a firm but fair disciplinarian and essentially a man of action. One of the war's earliest, and most urgent, calls for assistance received by the Marine Department was from the battleship HMS *Barham,* which had sustained serious mine damage. She managed to reach the Mersey approaches under her own power, but was so far down by the head that she was drawing 42 feet of water forward and only 18 feet aft. Hart realized that with such excessive draught there was no possibility of getting her into Gladstone Graving Dock, where she was to be repaired. His solution was to place a large number of pumps in the battleship's forward compartments and stack 1,200 tons of ballast on the after decking, which was shored from below to sustain the additional weight. This corrected her trim sufficiently for her to be docked. Among its many other tasks, the Marine Department had also brought in the crop of mine casualties previously described.

Hart got results and he was quite prepared to ride rough-shod over bureaucracy to achieve them. He was once visited by a senior civil servant from the Admiralty who disapproved of the heavy cost incurred, adding that further expenditure would have to be sanctioned by his department. Hart's trenchant reaction was that he was Liverpool's Salvage Officer, that he had received *carte blanche* from the Flag Officer in Charge, and that in these circumstances the civil servant's approval or otherwise was of no consequence whatever. The man left, never to be seen again.

Now, Hart and his men faced the most awesome challenge

of their careers. The German military theorist Clausewitz once commented that in war everything is simple, but that even the simplest operation is difficult. This exactly encapsulated the problems of the Marine Department. In simple terms it had to clear the wrecks, so freeing berths for incoming traffic. Each wreck, however, presented a different set of technical problems requiring decisions as to the equipment to be employed in the space available, the salvability of the cargo, whether the vessel could be repaired when raised and how to dispose of the hulk if she could not.

Some seventeen years after the event, Hart wrote in the *Liverpool Daily Post*:

> In all, more than forty wrecks of all types demanded our attention, and they included those of ten large vessels. Naturally, we could not tackle all these jobs at once. Our general rule was to give priority to vessels which would be repairable and to those which obstructed quay space or necessary channels. Even so, the task was complicated by the fact that, although the bombing had ceased, we were always liable to find ourselves faced with new emergencies which could not await our convenience. For instance, it was about this time, and while we were working on a tanker in the river, that we received an urgent summons to the destroyer HMS *Warwick,* mined and entering the Mersey in sinking condition. It was night time, there was a dense fog, and under ordinary conditions all navigation would have been entirely suspended, but in view of the imperative need of a destroyer at this period of the war, she was boarded by Commander Harbord and a party, who with great skill successfuly navigated the vessel to Tranmere, where she sank as she was beached. She was later repaired and returned to service.

In the docks themselves, Hart mobilized every man and vessel at his disposal. *Mammoth,* the great floating crane severely damaged in an earlier attack, was sorely missed, and so was her smaller sister *Hercules,* sunk in Langton Dock. A third member of the floating crane fleet, *Samson,* had been hit in the jib by a piece of the Overhead Railway when the *Malakand* blew up, but was quickly repaired. The following provides a representative selection of the work undertaken in the immediate aftermath of the enemy attack on the port.

Tug *Bison* (274 tons), sunk in Gladstone Dock - raised and repaired.

Cargo vessel *Roxburgh Castle* (7,801 tons), sunk in Alexandra Dock - refloated and repaired; cargo partly damaged by water.

Steam derrick barge *Rose* (143 tons), sunk in Alexandra Dock with a cargo of caustic soda aboard - cargo valued at £1,680 16s 8d salved by diver; engine and boilers salved; raised and broken up.

Cargo vessel *Domino* (1,453 tons), capsized and sunk in Canada Dock - cargo valued at £1218 8s 10d salved; constructive total loss; uprighted, raised and beached at Tranmere for breaking up.

Cargo vessel *Elstree Grange* (6,598 tons), burned out in Canada Dock - listed for breaking.

Light vessel *Sirius* (176 tons), sunk in Albert Dock raised and removed to Tranmere beach.

Passenger liner *Europa* (10,224 tons), burned out and sunk in Brocklebank Graving Dock - constructive total loss; patched, refloated and beached for breaking up.

Cargo vessel *Tacoma Star* (7,924), sunk in Canada Dock - refloated and repaired.

Floating crane *Hercules* (652 tons), sunk in Langton Dock; raised and repaired.

Cargo vessel *Baron Inchcape* (7,005 tons), down by the bows in Canada Dock with a cargo of oilcake pulse and grain aboard; vessel and cargo salved, the latter about forty per cent damaged by water. Hart comments: 'The swollen grain had almost plugged the leakage which, however, greatly increased with the discharge of cargo, and the vessel required continuous pumping to be kept afloat. Discharge proved a long and arduous process, as a great part of her cargo was under water and stank to high heaven, exuding such foul gasses as to make the use of gas masks imperative and cause all uniform gold lace to turn green.'

The invisible element of the damage inflicted by the enemy lay in the delay imposed on undamaged ships waiting to leave the port. Typical examples were the *Mercier* (7,886 tons) which, because of sheds destroyed by fire, was restricted to discharging overside and left eight days late; and *Melbourne Star* (12,806 tons), which was delayed for five days when she was forced to suspend discharge because of an unexploded bomb in the roadway opposite her berth. *Lobos* (6,479 tons)-was delayed for seventeen days because the cargo she had been about to embark lay buried under the rubble of a shed. This was, however, the worst example. Some ships left on time, others with only one or two days' delay; overall, delayed vessels spent an average of five additional days in port, a remarkable achievement in the circumstances.

The full extent of Liverpool's dramatic recovery is revealed by the weekly returns of tonnage landed throughout the period. During the week ended 26 April, the last full week before the attack, the figure was 181,562. By 3 May, after the attack had been in progress two days, it had fallen to 145,596 tons. On 10 May the full effects of the attack were revealed by a weekly landing total reduced to only 35,026 tons. Yet, incredibly, by 17 May the figure had risen to 85,678 tons, only 500 tons short of the landings during a slack week the previous month. On 24 May there was a slight reduction, but this merely reflected the fact that ships had been temporarily diverted to other ports until the emergency had passed. On 31 May the total had risen to 93,238 tons, and continued to rise - on 7 June it reached 108,773 tons and during the week ended 14 June no less than 126,936 tons were landed. To all intents and purposes, the port was working normally again. Eight days later, while the week's landing returns were being collated in the Dock Board offices, there came the dramatic news that the Wehrmacht had invaded the Soviet Union. The United Kingdom no longer stood alone and, however unlikely its ally, the general opinion was that this time Hitler had bitten off rather more than he could safely chew.

The destruction of shipping in the docks had amounted to the loss of a medium-sized convoy. The Royal Navy and the Ministry of War Transport were gravely concerned by this and both wrote to the Dock Board suggesting the dispersion of shipping in the event of enemy attack. Their suggestion was intended to be helpful, but it was not one with which the Dock Board felt it could concur. Ships were allocated berths appropriate to their cargoes, size and tonnage and a uniform dispersion was therefore not in itself appropriate. Furthermore, dispersion into the river would be a time-consuming exercise in which the tidal state and availability of tugs might not coincide with the enemy's attack; in fact, the disruption caused by such a measure would simply do the Luftwaffe's work for it by reducing the port's efficiency. Finally, if ships were to be sunk, it was better that they should go down in docks where they could be salved rather than in the river's main channels, where they would be a universal hindrance.

The validity of the last point was plain for all to see in the wreck of the *Ullapool*, lying off the Pier Head, where she constituted a serious navigational hazard. Captain Hart and his team quickly decided that she was too badly damaged to be salved and in the normal course of events would have dispersed her hulk across the river bed with a series of heavy explosive charges. Ullapool, however, was lying directly above the Mersey road and rail tunnels, damage to which could not be contemplated. Because of this, the strength of the charges had to be i limited and ten years were to pass before the last remnants of the wreck were scattered. Work on the *Tacoma City,* lying in a slightly less inconvenient situation off Rock Ferry, went on even longer. The ship had broken in half when she was mined and her two parts had drifted 800 feet apart before they sank, taking her 4,000-ton cargo of steel to the bottom. Diving teams had only succeeded in recovering 1,500 tons by the time the war ended and the residue was still being brought up as late as 1957.

If the Dock Board's monumental feat in restoring the port to normal engendered immense relief at Headquarters Western Approaches, Admiral Noble and his most senior colleagues also had grounds for intense jubilation, for on 9 May an event occurred which altered the complexion of the Battle of the Atlantic. On that day Convoy OB 318, which had left Liverpool a week earlier, was attacked by a submarine wolf-pack. During the action *U-110,* seriously damaged by the corvette *Aubretia's* depth charges, was forced to surface and was abandoned by her crew. A party from the destroyer *Bulldog* boarded her and returned with a priceless hoard of intelligence material, including radio frequencies, a naval Enigma coding machine, and its settings for several weeks ahead. This was one of the greatest coups of the war and remained so closely guarded a secret that no mention of it was made in the official history. By one of fate's strange coincidences, the U-boat's commander was Kapitanleutnant Fritz-Julius Lemp, the man who had sunk the *Athenia.* He was not among the survivors and one story has it that, realizing the submarine was in no immediate danger of sinking, he swam back to her, where he was shot dead by the boarding party. *U-110* foundered under tow the following day.

Air power was a major factor in the Battle of the Atlantic, particularly in those areas which could not initially be reached by land-based aircraft. Here the Germans began with an advantage, since their longrange Fw 200 Condors could prey on merchant shipping well beyond the range of fighter protection. To counter this menace the CAM (Catapult-Aircraft Merchant) ship was developed, armed with a single Hurricane which could be launched from a catapult ramp over the bows. Once launched, the fighter shot down or drove off the Condor, but was then forced to ditch beside a friendly vessel. The fighter pilots were trained in catapult-launch techniques at the RAF's Merchant Ship Fighter Unit, established at Speke on 5 May 1941 while the German attacks on Liverpool were still at their height. The CAM ships claimed a number of victims, but their principal value was deterrence.

An interim stage between the CAM ship and the fully developed escort carrier was the Merchant Aircraft Carrier (MAC). The MACs were either tankers or bulk carriers of over 8,000 tons with long, uncluttered upper decks, reinforced so that they could launch and recover aircraft. They carried up to four Swordfish torpedo bombers which, because of their low speed, were suitable for anti-submarine warfare. These remained on deck throughout the voyage. In other respects the vessels continued to perform their mercantile function and sailed under the Red Ensign. The MACs were conceived in 1942 and, because of Liverpool's excellent bulk handling facilities, were to be seen regularly in the port during the latter half of the war.

Liverpool's ordeal and astonishing recovery had attracted the admiration of the national leadership. In October 1941 King George VI paid his third visit to the port, and returned in October the following year with Queen Elizabeth. Never physically strong, he had assumed the burdens of the monarchy and of the war without hesitation and he and his family had deliberately remained in London to share the danger with their people. His quiet sense of duty, his understanding, sympathy and kindness won him the highest regard, both as a king and as a man. When touring Liverpool he made a point of talking personally to those who had been bereaved or who had lost their homes, and sometimes a shaken hand would be left in possession of a bank note; the probability is that it was never spent.

Winston Churchill, deeply concerned for the survival of the port, had been in Liverpool on 25 April and returned later in the year to witness its recovery for himself. In peacetime, many of the dockers held quite different political views from his own, but now they recognized a war leader of rare genius. They cheered and took off their caps to him. He beamed and took off his hat to them. 'I see the damage done by the enemy attacks,' he commented, 'but I also see, side by side with the devastation, and amid the ruins, quiet, confident, bright and smiling eyes, beaming with consciousness of being associated with a cause far higher and wider than any of human or personal issue. I see the spirit of an unconquered people.'

Another visitor was the world-renowned Irish tenor, Count John McCormack, who, on 20 October, gave one of the last public performances of his life before a huge crowd of appreciative workers at Gladstone Dock.

Meanwhile, steps were being taken to strengthen the city's defences in case the Luftwaffe should return. The first of these was largely administrative and involved the absorption of the Liverpool Fire Brigade into the National Fire Service (NFS) as Fire Force No. 26 on 18 August 1941. Forty men of the Liverpool Brigade and its associated AFS units had lost their lives as a result of enemy action, and reinforcement brigades had also sustained serious casualties. Even when their own city was not under attack, Liverpool firemen had been in action in other areas under pressure, including Manchester and Belfast. The loss of identity was sad, but given that the problem itself was national in scale, a national solution was essential.

The second step was the formation of the first of the so-called Z batteries in October 1941. These were armed with rockets, known as unrotated projectiles (UP), incorporating a high-explosive warhead. They were of 3-inch calibre and were six feet long, being fired in salvoes from twenty-four projectors. It was hoped that the sheer volume of their output would compensate for inaccuracy when they blanketed the area above a target with their bursts, but their maximum effective ceiling was too low to provide anything other than a deterrent. Because of the danger from falling fins and propellant tubes, they were primarily used in defence of dock areas and sited where they could be fired over water; the battery covering the south docks were located in Sefton Park and that covering the north docks in New Brighton. In this context, warships in port supplemented the land-based anti-aircraft defences as a matter of course. On one occasion a cruiser, having only solid armour-piercing rounds left in her magazine, decided to send them up anyway; their trajectory took them several miles into the stratosphere from whence they fell to earth around the village of Parbold, near Ormskirk, provoking understandable discussion.

The third step was to erect three anti-aircraft forts in the outer reaches of the Mersey estuary, where they could break up enemy formations before they reached the port and prevent minelaying in the main channels. The idea of such forts had been conceived by a prominent civil engineer, Mr G.A. Maunsell, early in the war, and received the Admiralty's approval. It was envisaged that the forts would contain heavy and light anti-aircraft weapons, a searchlight position, radar, generators, stores, fuel tanks and accommodation for the garrison. The space required was considerable and it was decided that each fort would consist of seven towers interconnected by high walkways. The towers themselves consisted of a hollow reinforced concrete base from which rose four similarly constructed legs surmounted by a concrete cap into which were embedded the joists supporting a triple-decked steel barracks and gun platform; the last mounted either one 3.7-inch gun, or two light Bofors guns, or a searchlight, plus radar and range-finding equipment as appropriate. The towers were prefabricated and as each was completed it was towed out to its site, slung between two specially constructed pontoons, and then lowered to the sea bed in the correct position relative to the other towers of the fort.

One factor which influenced the design and construction of the forts was that in the days following Dunkirk conventional shipyard space, labour and material were simply not available, and since they were urgently required the situation demanded unconventional solutions. A construction site was established at the south end of Lever Brothers' Bromborough Dock property, and the work itself was carried out not by shipbuilders, but by the Cleveland Bridge and Engineering Company. Siting the forts was in itself a difficult problem, as the estuary was notoriously exposed, being subject to strong tidal flows, and its bed consisted of treacherous and constantly moving sand. After hydrographic surveys, however, three sites were selected and as the 117-feet-high towers were completed they were towed out and emplaced by Captain Hart's Marine Department between the end of 1942 and the middle of 1943. Formby AA towers (Fort No. 1) lay some four miles off Formby Point; Queen's AA Towers (Fort No. 2) were situated north-east of the Bar lightship and covered the northern flank of the Queen's Channel; Burbo AA Towers (Fort No.3) were located on the edge of Burbo Bank and covered the southern flank of the Queen's Channel.

The forts were the responsibility of Anti-Aircraft Command, and General Pile commented that had they existed during the period of German attacks the damage sustained by Merseyside would have been considerably reduced. Together, the new forts and the latest radar-equipped night fighters would have made further attacks an expensive business. As it was, they never fired their guns in anger. Life for their garrisons was inevitably dull and in winter they were marooned in a wind-lashed world of broken water, having to wait up to eighteen days for water, provisions, mail and relief. Medical attention was not always available for serious cases and on one occasion a man died of peritonitis, despite the intervention of the New Brighton lifeboat. Sometimes, when severe gales buffeted the towers, men thought they were moving; they were. For these reasons, coupled with the unlikelihood of further German attacks, the forts were never fully manned.

Old hands on the river had always doubted the feasibility of erecting such structures in the estuary, and in the long term they were proved right. In considering the question of scour, the hydrographic surveyors were instructed to concentrate on tidal effects and ignore those of wave motion. This proved to be a fundamental mistake in an area where waves measuring thirty feet from crest to trough were commonplace. Furthermore, the sand itself, being Liverpool sand, had a mind of its own, did not consider itself subject to the normal rules of nature, and would sometimes run uphill in apparent defiance of gravity. The result was that the scour around the towers was uneven and, over a period, they began to lean into the trenches formed. After the war, they became unsafe and were taken down.

The story of the Maunsell forts provides a reminder that, whatever the state of hostilities, the perils of the sea remained constant. Fog, gales and reduced navigation lighting all conspired to drive vessels ashore on the treacherous shoals, one of the most notable examples being the steamer *Pegu,* completely wrecked on the Crosby Revetment during the first months of the war; over 100 of her passengers and crew were saved by the New Brighton lifeboat.

While Liverpool slowly returned to normality and its defences were strengthened, distant events were again to have a profound effect on the port's contribution to the national war effort. John Winant had replaced the isolationist Joseph Kennedy as the United States ambassador to Great Britain, and he was far more positive in his approach than his gloomy predecessor. Committed to establishing the closest possible relationship between the two countries, he got out and about among the people and soon became an extremely popular figure. On 26 November 1941 he was in Liverpool, watching dockers unload Lease-Lend cargoes. 'You'll soon be seeing the old Stars and Stripes coming across,' he told them. It was a prophetic remark, for on 7 December Japanese carrier aircraft launched an unprovoked attack on the American naval base at Pearl Harbor and suddenly the United States had become a combatant. For the first time, doubts regarding the ultimate outcome of the war were dispelled, for the Axis powers were now confronted by the resources of the British Empire, the industrial might of America and the immense manpower of the Soviet Army; if Japan's entry into the war meant that the task would take a little longer, so be it. More was to be demanded of Liverpool than at any time in its history and, because of the Luftwaffe's failure to destroy the port, Liverpool was able to respond.

6

Living With It

The war had over three years to run, and before dealing with the port's continued effort it is worth recalling something of life in the city during that period. For a boy, it was a most exciting place in which to grow up. Time soon healed some of the more horrific memories of the Blitz, although many would never be forgotten, including returning from the shelter to find my pillow skewered to the mattress by a long scimitar of window glass. There was, however, so much of interest to occupy the mind that each day brought a new discovery.

In the river, for example, there were ships of every shape and kind, the majority painted uniform grey. There were aircraft carriers, cruisers, destroyers, frigates, corvettes, armed trawlers and minesweepers; there were ocean liners with famous names now serving as troopships, bulk carriers, tankers, freighters, tramps and the new mass-produced Liberty ships, all mounting poop guns for self-defence; there were white-painted hospital ships, clearly marked with red crosses, cross-channel ferries, coasters, tugs by the score, flats, dredgers, pilot boats, salvage vessels and floating cranes There were the masts and upperworks of sunken ships and there were large green-painted wreck buoys to mark the graves of vanished vessels. And always, plying through and around the shipping in the crowded fairway, there were the Birkenhead, Seacombe and New Brighton ferries, punctual and totally reliable. Quite unconsciously, one learned the workings of a great port, to recognize the different types of ships, the meanings of the flags they flew and the language of the mariner. If one was unsure of something, one could ask the next man along and, because Liverpool was wedded to the sea, the chances were that he could provide the answer.

Above the city the balloon barrage still floated, now close-hauled save for testing, but of greater interest were the growing numbers of RAF fighters, bombers and training aircraft which flew overhead and, again, one learned aircraft recognition subconsciously. These were later joined by the less familiar shapes of aircraft manned by the US Army Air Force. Sometimes, there was the sound of machine-gun and cannon fire offshore and it was assumed, correctly, that pilots were perfecting their strafing techniques in the estuary; unfortunately, some of the more exuberant among them selected the main-channel marker buoys as their targets. Captain Hart was furious, but the culprits were never caught.

Ashore, the stream of land-warfare weapons to and from the docks provided continuous interest. As D Day approached, the general direction of the flow was inwards from the United States. Much of this movement took place at night with the heavy weapons, including tanks and artillery, travelling on heavily sheeted trains to secret destinations in southern England. Latterly, the railways became so burdened that tanks left the docks on their own tracks, creating an ear-splitting, windowrattling racket as they roared over the cobbles on the roads out of the city. More common were the apparently endless convoys of American lorries, some flying red flags to indicate they were carrying ammunition, shepherded by military police motor-cyclists.

The city centre was always crowded with servicemen and women on leave or duty. Amid the throng there were men from Canada, France, Belgium, Holland, Norway, Czechoslovakia and Poland, a moving kaleidoscope of peaked caps, forage caps, berets, kepis, Polish mortar boards, French pom-poms, naval cap ribbons, uniform khaki, dark or light blue, polished Sam Browne belts, gleaming brass buttons, gold lace, medal ribbons, service insignia and badges of rank. Early in 1942 the crowd was swelled by a growing number of Americans.

Although they shared a common language, at this period the average Briton and American knew comparatively little of each other, and both suffered from a number of somewhat negative preconceived ideas which would take a little time to dispel. This was less true in Liverpool than the majority of places, partly because of the port's historical connections with the United States, partly because a high percentage of the seafaring populations had actually visited America, and partly because Liverpool had always accepted a stranger on his merits rather than on his background. The Americans were friendly, good company and, as far as children were concerned, generous to a fault. A booklet was produced for those stationed in the area, describing places of interest with particular relevance to the port's transatlantic associations, and the newcomers could often be seen with this, tracing the route followed by their emigrant grandparents.

Not that all was sweetness and light. The arrival of thousands of fit, healthy young men provided serious competition for female company. In this connection the Americans had something of an edge, since they were well paid by British standards, had smarter uniforms and access to such luxuries as nylon stockings. Naturally, wishing to impress, they shot formidable and quite unverifiable lines. It was astonishing just how many Texas oil millionaires, Western cattle barons and Detroit motor magnates had chosen to serve in the ranks, more often than not in the same infantry platoon or bomber crew; equally astonishing was the number of people who believed them. The city's queens of the night also found themselves competing with a crowd of very undesirable incomers seeking easy money and good time. All in all, the receipe for trouble may have seemed complete, but it was further compounded by a very sour element. At this period the US Army employed what amounted to a policy of segregation with regard to its black troops, the majority of whom were employed in service units. At home, many of the black soldiers were subject to a rigid code of discrimination in which relationships with white women were an absolute taboo and they were pleased to find this did not apply to quite the same extent in the United Kingdom. Unfortunately, they were often the focus of dance-hall fights, the causes of which were invariably women, their opponents being either local men or white Americans. These fracas were quickly broken up, often with the assistance of the American military police, who were uncompromising in the use of their night sticks

What alarmed the Chief Constable most about this was that, somehow, the normally industrious and lawabiding Chinese community were dragged in to the point that a blood feud between them and coloured people generally, including their indigenous neighbours, seemed in the offing. The immediate cause is known to have been a dispute over white women, and it seems probable that one or more members of the community had been killed or seriously injured in the type of brawl described above. By judicious policing, the situation was contained.

Troubles of this kind were, fortunately, the exception rather than the rule. Most servicemen visiting Liverpool simply wanted to relax and enjoy their free time, and the city did its best to make them feel welcome by providing accommodation and clubs. Provision for the Merchant Navy already existed at the officers' club in Percy Street, the Gordon Smith Institute for Seamen, the Liverpool Sailors' Home, and Plimsoll House in Gambier Terrace, but in October 1942 the brand new Ocean Club was opened in Lord Street for personnel of the Royal and Merchant Navies and the WRNS. Two floors of the old North Western Hotel in Lime Street became a club for officers of the armed services, who could also obtain accommodation in the Racquets Club in Upper Parliament Street. Other clubs providing accommodation, canteens, bars, libraries, rest rooms and entertainment were the Liverpool United Service Club, the Angel Services Club in Dale Street, the Allied Centre in Basnett Street, the Ranelagh Services Club and YMCA in Church Street, the Welsh Services Club in Upper Parliament Street, the Salvation Army, the Church Army, Toc H and the Knights of St Columba; for those who simply wanted to get away from it all for a few hours there'was the Services Quiet Club, located in the old Royal Institution Building in Colquitt Street. The Americans could obtain accommodation at the Dorchester Hotel in Rodney Street or at the Palace Services Club in Birkdale, but reserved a hostel situated at 102 - 104 Whitechapel for their black troops. Rotarians found friends among the local clubs and Masons among the local lodges. There were plenty of families, too, who were glad to treat a serviceman to a meal and a comfortable bed in their own homes. Most places of entertainment, including footballs clubs, dance halls, cinemas and theatres, reduced their admission charges for personnel in uniform; it was, for example, possible to listen to a concert of international standard at the Philharmonic Hall for as little as one shilling. Even tram conductors, many of them veterans of World War I, declined to take the serviceman's proffered fare unless an inspector was about.

There was one occasion, however, when Liverpool's fondness for the services got somewhat out of hand. The Army announced that in September 1942 it intended mounting a major invasion exercise in the city, and since this would involve street fighting it requested that the population should stay indoors. The choice was a bad one in that it completely ignored the streak of good-humoured perversity in the Liverpool character. The event received so much cautionary publicity in the press and in repeated announcements in schools that the enthusiasm generated was quite uncontrollable. People wanted to see *their* soldiers in action, and nothing was going to stop them. When the great day dawned and the troops began moving into position they were soon halted by genial crowds. It was a wonderful opportunity for the grizzled veterans of Mons, of Ypres and the Somme, of Gallipoli, Palestine and Mesopotamia, and even of Spion Kop, Ladysmith and Kimberley, to emphasize their status, and they beset senior officers, many of whom also wore World War I ribbons, offering plentiful advice, old soldiers' wisdom and reminiscences galore. Elsewhere, orders groups were penetrated by unofficial civilian observers, ready with helpful street directions; machine-gun and mortar teams were required to explain the workings of their weapons; tracked carrier crews were forced to suspend operations and drink cups of tea; snipers attempting total concealment were surrounded by admiring groups; and small boys offered both sides their services as spies. The police did their best to disperse the throngs, but they might as well have attempted to control a fog. At length, the generals bowed to the inevitable and withdrew. As an exercise, the day had been a disaster; as an essay in public relations, it had been wonderful.

Daily life had resumed an established pattern. Unless they were already fully employed, civilians were required to perform some form of war work, the only exceptions being children, the elderly, invalids and those who looked after them. My father voluntarily abandoned his career with the Liverpool Philharmonic Orchestra to make machine tools; other members of the family worked at MC5 or in local departments of the War Of fice. Thanks to the fair rationing system, no one went hungry. Luxury foods had long since vanished, but the fare was plain and healthy ănd could be supplemented by such items as rabbit, whalemeat and snoek (a fish normally rejected by trawlermen during peacetime). A few hens, kept in the back yard, produced additional eggs. Of the more common vegetables there was never a shortage and people were encouraged to grow more in their own gardens or in allotments provided for the purpose. There were usually apples, pears and plums to be had in season, but there was a shortage of tropical fruits; bananas vanished almost completely and when a shipment did arrive it was strictly allocated on the basis of one banana per child. Sweets and chocolates were also strictly rationed and such things as liquorice root provided a poor substitute. Occasionally, teachers would distribute boxes of candy, the gift of thoughtful American schools, and American servicemen usually had the odd stick of chewing gum to offer. Ice cream was a distant memory.

Clothing was undoubtedly drab, but serviceable. Good, pre-war clothes were saved for special occasions, put safely away with a few mothballs in the pockets, or restyled with the aid of patterns when they had passed their best. In their place there was dull, hard-wearing Utility clothing, rationed like everything else. Ladies' hats, once *de rigueur,* were reserved for weddings and replaced by turbans or headscarves. Boys everywhere wore what amounted to a basic uniform consisting of grey angola shirt, grey pullover, grey flannel or worsted shorts held up by an elastic belt with a snake buckle, and grey socks.

At home, women knitted an endless stream of sweaters, scarves, gloves, socks and Balaclava helmets for their menfolk in the services and, while the needles clicked, everyone listened to the radio. The BBC's reputation never stood higher than during the war years, when the Corporation's unquestioned patriotism was combined with a profound integrity in reporting the news, be it good or bad, earning it the complete trust of all. By way of contrast, one could listen to the extravagant claims of the traitor William Joyce, better known as Lord Haw Haw because of his assumed upper-class accent, broadcasting from Germany. It was said that Joyce had once lived in Liverpool, and he was heartily detested. His purpose was to demoralize but he merely enraged. Captured in 1945, he was tried and executed the following year.

Daily, the telegraph boys cycled by with their grim tidings of men killed, wounded or missing in action. Daily, postmen brought letters from those on active service and emptied pillar boxes crammed with family news for absent fathers, husbands and brothers. Sometimes, a printed card would arrive from a German, Italian or Japanese prison camp; it told the recipient little, save that the sender was alive at the time of posting, up to a year earlier. For young mothers, the work of bringing up a family without the man of the house was hard and often exasperating. Sadly, the strain of enforced separation proved too much for some marriages, on one side or the other.

Occasionally, there would be brutal fights when a serviceman, warned by neighbours of his wife's misconduct, would return home unexpectedly to sort out her fancy man. Relief from tension could be found in the local pub, where lusty sing-songs around the piano would continue outside long after the landlord had locked the instrument and shouted 'Time, gentlemen, PLEASE!' Often, the goodhumoured revellers, arms round each others' shoulders for mutual support, would stagger home, still singing, and sometimes, in the blackout, one would trip over a kerb and they would all fall. The cut knees and bloodied noses would result in wide-ranging recriminations which were never less than interesting.

Grocers' shops also became unofficial social centres on which housewives converged whenever a fresh allocation of scarce commodities arrived. There the local gossip and news could be exchanged beneath cautionary posters which proclaimed 'WALLS HAVE EARS!' From time to time, grocers were able to accumulate small surpluses which were distributed quietly to their best customers, the package being placed in the shopping basket without a word and as silently added to the bill. These dealings were referred to as being 'under the counter,' but were entirely legal. If the grocer was a good businessman he would wait until his surplus was large enough to supply the majority of his customers with a little bit extra, and then, following an exchange of worldly-wise winks, they would all go on their way believing they had a special relationship with him.

However, grocers too had their problems. In those days prepackaging was almost unknown and bulk commodities such as tea and sugar were delivered in chests and sacks. They were then weighed out into bags in front of the customer and, since the package always weighed marginally more than the statutory measure, the overall effect was to produce a shortfall in the grocer's stock, which could only be renewed by supplying the appropriate number of ration coupons. Ultimately, a situation could arise in which he could not discharge the legal requirement to supply the rations due to his registered customers.

The prospect of this had begun to haunt the dreams of Tom Griffiths, the proprietor of the Bedford Stores, for he was rapidly running out of tea. One of his staff mentioned that they had been approached by black marketeers who would willingly make good the shortfall, but Griffiths, a man of impeccable character, was utterly opposed to dealing with such people. At length the situation became so desperate that he felt he had no alternative and, visiting the address he had been given, was shown tea chests apparently containing good-quality tea. He agreed to purchase three at the exorbitant price of £30, payable on delivery. These duly arrived, but the suppliers were apparently unsettled by the alleged presence of a police car in the neighbourhood and left quickly, commenting that they wouldn't stop to count their money as Griffiths was obviously a gentleman Needless to say, when the chests were opened in the stockroom they contained nothing but sawdust and other rubbish. Feeling that his foray into the underworld had merited its own punishment, Griffiths nonetheless advised a friend in the police. Since there were no regulations governing the purchase of boxed sawdust by respectable citizens, the officer was inclined to agree, but set in motion an investigation which resulted in the arrest of the entrepreneurs in Leeds.

By far the most common form of public entertainment was the cinema. An entire column, and sometimes more, of the *Liverpool Echo's* front page was devoted to cinema advertisements. There were cinemas all over the city, varying from the grandly opulent in the centre, through the comfortable in the respectable suburbs, to the 'laugh and scratch' fleapits somewhere in between. The newest films were shown first in the city centre and, during the next few weeks, worked their way out to the suburbs. Many people went to the cinema at least once a week and some went to see films like *Gone With The Wind, Mrs Miniver* and *In Which We Serve*, time and again. Queues were commonplace. On Saturday mornings or afternoons there were children's matinees, for which the price of admission was 3d (lp). The cinema was, therefore, a most important channel of communication between the Government and the people and programmes included official announcements as well as newsreels showing the progress of the war on all fronts.

There were fewer theatres, but they were all well attended and, in the main, concentrated on revues and variety shows which provided a cheerful night out. Live entertainment was also introduced in industrial canteens during meal breaks, giving many people a unique opportunity to see some of the great personalities of show business at close quarters. It was the custom of the times that at such shows, real appreciation was demonstrated not merely by applause, but also by shrill, sustained whistling, accorded whether the artistes were stand-up comics or classical quartets. The BBC toured the country, broadcasting these performances under the title of *Workers' Playtime,* and there was no doubt that they were genuinely appreciated.

Such were the commonplaces of everday conversation, brightened occasionally by the news of a man's promotion or decoration for gallantry, or joy at the prospect of his impending leave. When he was granted leave, he somehow found himself spending it in uniform, for the benefit of his girlfiend or family, who were proud of him and wished everyone to know it.

The child's world was much simpler, and in many ways the childhood of those who grew up during the war years had more in common with that of their Victorian grandparents than with the middle of the twentieth century. There were, for example, few commercially produced toys. One could browse through pre-war issues of the *Meccano Magazine,* looking wistfully at the array of superb die-cast Dinky models and the Hornby train sets, and plan what to buy when better times arrived; in the meantime, the factory was fully engaged with other matters, and one had to accept that better times meant that ill-defined area of the future known as 'after the war'. There were, however, model aeroplane and other kits made from preshaped balsa-wood parts, and with a degree of effort a reasonable result could be achieved with these. Rag dolls had replaced their more sophisticated sisters of the 1930s, but girls enjoyed dressing them just as much. Since there was no television service, reading for pleasure was far more commonplace then, and there was no shortage of books and weekly comics to suit every taste. Apart from these more personal pastimes and the organized sports at school, children could also join youth organizations such as the Boy Scouts or Girl Guides. Most of our time was spent outside, playing timeless street games such as tick in all its versions, hopscotch, marbles, jinks, whipping tops, bowling hoops and, in the autumn, conkers. Then, of course, there was mischief, the native bucko wildness often going uncurbed because of the absence of fathers in the services. This could take the form of practical jokes played on adults in the hope it would provoke pursuit, or doing what was forbidden because it was obviously dangerous and therefore conferred status. Typical of this was "skippin' leckies" (riding on the buffers or steps of tramcars until chased off by the conductor) or "skippin' ellers" (hanging off the tailboard of an LMS delivery vehicle powered by a three-wheel mechanical horse). When Lewis's rebuilt their department store, they placed below the statue of Liverpool Resurgent a panel showing a pack of ragamuffins in full cry, and it captured the spirit of the times exactly.

There was, inevitably, a darker side to life, as there was in any city. In his report on the war years the Chief Constable commented that between 1938 and 1945 offences against property involving violence had risen three-fold. The term violence is relative, however, and vicious assaults were rare. Despite Liverpool's reputation as a tough town, the criminal use of firearms was virtually unknown, mugging had yet to be invented and drugs were taken solely for medicinal purposes. Bank cashiers did not require the protection of bullet-proof screens. Football supporters would have regarded as astonishing the suggestion that one day they would be segregated and penned behind iron fences. Rape and attacks on children and the elderly were infrequent and despised even by hardened criminals, who often exacted their own brutal vengeance. Most organized thefts were the work of black marketeers, who could supply anything at a price, or deserters attempting to support themselves. Spivs, the front men of the Black Market, were curious creatures who had somehow evaded service, generally on spurious medical grounds. It might be thought that they sought anonymity, but they openly advertised their role as illicit providers by wearing large trilbies, flashy suits with shoulder pads and gaudy ties. Some the authorities tolerated as little fishes because of the information they produced, but others suddenly found themselves directed into dirty and time-consuming regular employment.

More dangerous were the organized gangs which frequented the less reputable areas, and these the police spared no efforts to break up. Penalties included hanging, hard labour and corporal punishment. One gang member, a habitual criminal, was sentenced to a term of imprisonment and eighteen strokes for refusing to go to sea. The Chief Constable might comment that law enforcement was regarded by some sections of the community as a sort of contest between themselves and the police, but the fact was that it was undeniably a simpler matter then than it is today. During the course of the war Liverpool police officers were awarded eleven George Medals, nine British Empire Medals, including one Bar, and one Belgian Croix de Guerre, the majority for rescues from bomb-damaged property or the removal of ammunition from burning dock sheds or ships. The Liverpool Shipwreck and Humane Society also made numerous awards to officers for rescues from drowning or fires and for halting runaway horses.

As mentioned earlier, much of the docks traffic remained horse-drawn, and the horse still played a major part in the city's domestic life. For short-haul work, involving constant stopping and starting, the horse was and in some circumstances remains more economic than motor transport, and was used by brewers, coal merchants and milkmen. The city's refuse was also collected by horse-drawn wagons, but the system was partially merchanized in that motor transporters winched full wagons aboard and deposited empty wagons for the teams during the course of their rounds. Many motor lorries towed a trailer for the sake of fuel economy and some haulage companies managed to remain competitive by prolonging the lives of their elderly steam wagons. There were comparatively few private cars to be seen on the streets. Those that were still running belonged to doctors and others whose work justified an allocation of petrol; the remainder had long since been laid up by their owners.

Holidays were a problem, partly because so many resorts, their beaches covered with barbed-wire entanglements and concrete dragon's teeth, their hotels requisitioned as billets, had ceased to function as such, and partly because, commuting apart, travelling on the overburdened railways was officially discouraged. On the other hand, the authorities had no wish to diminish the value of long-awaited summer breaks any more than was necessary, and to this end the Holidays at Home scheme was evolved. The parks became the focus of band concerts, displays, open-air theatre and entertainments of every kind, all available at nominal cost, and were more densely used than at any time in their history; for its part the Council agreed that they might also be used for 'suitable' games on Sundays. Liverpool people were additionally fortunate in that New Brighton and Southport still had open beaches, swimming facilities, permanent fairgrounds, donkey rides and many other attractions. Of the two, New Brighton attracted the greater number of day trippers from the city, the voyage down-river and back being considered an important part of the outing. From the deck of the crowded ferry it was possible to see the bustling life of the river, exchange waves with men lining the rails of outward-bound troopships at the Landing Stage, and look across the water at the Liverpool streets lying beneath the grey-brown blanket exuded by thousands of coal fires The sun shone and the salt breeze off the Irish Sea contained a whiff of something that had been absent during the first half of the war; it was optimism.

6

Winning Through

The measure of Liverpool's contribution to eventual victory is best understood by examining the statistics involved. During the six years of war 120,000,000 tons of ocean-going shipping passed through the port, an average of over 13,000 vessels per annum. The annual figure dropped steadily until 1942, when 14,242,812 tons were recorded, but thereafter rose steadily, reaching 20,099,500 tons in 1945. In addition, there was an overall total of 23,000,000 tons of coastal shipping. The inflationary effects of the war resulted in a sustained rise in dues received by the Dock Board, the figure for 1945 being £4,240,251 some sixty per cent more than in the comparable year of 1939 despite the fact that 1,700,000 tons fewer were harboured.

Cargo landed amounted to 56,494,800 tons, including the following:

Food- 19,000,000 tons
Fuel oil and petrol - 5,750,000 tons
Iron and steel - 3,701,030 tons
Non-ferrous metals - 2,585,190 tons
Timber - 2,497,700 tons
Cotton- 1,701,075 tons
Chemicals - 795,085 tons
Tanks, other military vehicles and spares - 66,000 tons

Aircraft and spares - 659,390 tons
Machinery - 341,840 tons
Manufactured goods - 267,489 tons
Miscellaneous war cargo -1,218,930 tons

The great bulk of this presented no problem other than sheer hard work, but aircraft, because of their shape, were awkward to handle. The majority arrived as deck cargo and to ease the burden the floating cranes, which were in constant demand, an ingenious solution was devised. Three of the old vehicle ferries, which had faced eventual extinction when the Mersey road tunnel was opened, were fitted with Scotch derricks and used to unload vessels in mid-river, their flat decks each being able to accommodate several aircraft. Of the 73,782 aircraft and gliders landed, over 11,000 were brought ashore in this way. The converted ferries were also used to take off tanks and other unwieldy items of deck cargo.

Despite the damage caused by the Luftwaffe, the docks' capacity to handle cargo increased appreciably. By 1944 the Dock Board had thirty-six steam locomotives in operation, a fifty per cent increase on the pre-war figure, and the capacity of railway wagon sidings had almost tripled to 3,185 vehicles. An additional 260 mobile cranes had also been brought into service. Space within the dock estate's warehouses was seriously reduced by enemy action, the requirements of the Royal Navy and, later, by those of the US Army, which requisitioned 149,000 square yards. On the other hand, the lessons of the enemy attacks of British ports had been learned and the Ministry of War Transport decided that in order to minimize the risk to incoming cargoes, they should be transported quickly by rail or road to inland depots where they could be sorted in safety for onward despatch. Work on Liverpool's depot, situated at Kirkby, then a small village, began in September 1941 and was completed a year later. It consisted of four large sheds served by nineteen miles of sidings connected to the Liverpool Exchange-Manchester main line, and occupied no less than ninety-seven acres.

Cargo despatched abroad from the port amounted

to 18,655,300 tons. This included tanks, guns, aircraft and war stores of all kinds bound for every theatre of war in which British troops were engaged, military aid for the Soviet Union, and such manufactured goods as were still being made for export. Many of the ships forming part of the hard-fought Malta relief convoys were loaded on Merseyside, as was much of the vast logistic support armada required for Operation Torch, the AngloAmerican landings in French North Africa, and for Operation Overlord, the D Day landings on the coast of Normandy.

Concurrently, Liverpool's unrivalled passenger handling facilities were working at full capacity. Over 4,700,000 troops passed through, including 1,200,000 Americans, the busiest period being during Operation Bolero, the transatlantic shipment of troops and equipment prior to the Allied invasion of Europe. Riverside Station, which in the palmy days of luxury ocean travel had handled up to four trains a week, sometimes despatched one train an hour for thirty hours at a stretch. Altogether, 2,133 trains carrying 752,039 disembarked troops left Riverside for destinations throughout the country, and 2,515 trains carrying 995,336 troops for embarkation arrived at the station. Often, troops were able to embark or disembark using the permanent gangways of the Landing Stage, but when this was occupied they were transported to and from anchored troopships by means of the vehicle ferries.

The tramcar also proved itself to be an excellent vehicle for troop transport since, unlike the bus, loading and unloading could be carried out from both ends. Long convoys of trams carried troops from the Pier Head to the main railway stations and transit camps on the outskirts of the city, or in the reverse direction. The efficiency of the system was demonstrated by the fact that all the occupants of a troop train could be loaded aboard a fleet of waiting trams and be on the move within ten minutes of the train reaching a station. At times, notably during the embarkation for Operation Torch, as many as 200 trams were employed in this way, and they were also used to distribute rations in bulk to the transit camps. These movements took place at night and their full extent remained secret until the war in Europe was over. Earlier in the war, trams were used to transport alien internees under guard from the stations to the Pier Head, whence they were shipped to camps in the Isle of Man.

Less obvious, but equally important, was the port's infrastructure, which also remained under constant pressure. Amid the intense activity of loading and unloading, ships required bunkering, victualling and repairing, tasks complicated by the fact that, in addition to merchant vessels, the Royal Navy might have as many as 200 ships of various types in port. Special arrangements had to be made for hospital ships and vessels carrying repatriated prisoners of war; the latter had been released by the enemy under a scheme supervised by the International Red Cross which permitted the exchange of officers and men too sick or badly wounded to be fit for further military service. The first of these ships, the *Atlantis,* entered the Mersey in October 1943 with 800 former prisoners aboard, to be welcomed by the sirens of every vessel in the river. She was followed in 1944 by the Swedish liner *Drottningholm,* whose passengers included civilian repatriates. Understandably, their arrival at the Landing Stage produced moving scenes, only to be equalled in the months after the war when ships carrying former prisoners of the Japanese, many still showing the physical and mental scars of their ordeal, began reaching Liverpool.

As preparations for the Allied invasion of Europe continued, Merseyside became closely involved in numerous top-secret projects, including Pluto, an acronym for Pipeline Under The Ocean. In April 1942 Lord Louis Mountbatten, then Chief of Combined Operations, sought technical advice on the feasibility of laying a fuel pipeline across the Channel. Early tests showed that it could be done, but the real breakthrough came when it was discovered that a three-inch steel pipe could be welded to any required length and still retain sufficient flexibility for it to be wound onto a drum not less than thirty feet in diameter. It was decided, therefore, that the pipeline would be laid from huge floating drums known as conundrums which could be towed across the Channel. Each conundrum was ninety feet long, over fifty feet in diameter, and carried seventy miles of pipeline.

Pluto actually began at two tanker mooring buoys off Bromborough. From these the oil was pumped ashore to balancing tanks and then to the main storage tanks up river at Stanlow, impelled by two large electric pumps, one of 1,000 hp and the other of 800 hp, with a total capacity of 1,200 tons per hour. At Stanlow the oil entered the main pipeline network, which included a feeder line from the terminal of Avonmouth, being pumped and boosted along its journey to the south coast. During the final months of the war Pluto carried one million gallons a day across the Channel by means of sixteen pipelines laid between Dungeness and Boulogne and four between the Isle of Wight and Cherbourg, and thence to the Rhine.

Bromborough shore also witnessed invasion preparations of a different sort. In the aftermath of the Dieppe raid in 1942 the Allies recognized that when they returned to the continent of Europe they could not rely on the early capture of a harbour in working order. It was decided, therefore, that two artificial harbours would be constructed off the Normandy beach-head, one on the British sector at Arromanches and the other on the American sector at St Laurent, the prefabricated components of these being towed across the Channel Codenamed Mulberries, the harbours consisted of offshore and flanking breakwaters constructed with large ferro-concrete caissons, some the size of five-storey buildings, which were towed into position and sunk, supplemented by blockships. Within the areas of water so enclosed each harbour contained three floating piers, connected to the shore by floating roadways.

Many of the caissons were built at Bromborough,

the task being rendered difficult by the residue of tidal mud deposited in their inner sections, which were hosed clean twice daily by an NFS detachment. They were completed in April 1944 and towed south to their invasion assembly area. The emplacement of the Mulberries, the towing of the Pluto conundrums and numerous other invasion tasks, involved every tug in the river, and indeed every tug in the country, supplemented by more from the United States. Unfortunately, between 18 and 22 June 1944, both harbours were severely damaged by the worst gale recorded for forty years, the American Mulberry so badly that it was never brought into service. The effect of this was to delay the Allied build-up and the fact that the Americans were eventually able to land more vehicles, equipment and supplies across open beaches than could be handled by the repaired British harbour led to criticism of the concept. On balance, however, the majority agreed that it was worthwhile, if only for the sheltered water provided by the breakwaters and the relative ease with which the British were able to land difficult loads.

From this sustained level of activity, the only possible conclusion which can be drawn is that the German failure to destroy Liverpool was tantamount in its effects to a major defeat in the field, comparable with the destruction of the Axis armies in Africa or the surrender at Stalingrad. As a naval base and headquarters Liverpool was, too, to achieve victory in what was for the Allies the most important campaign of the war, the Battle of the Atlantic.

On 19 November 1942 Admiral Sir Percy Noble, who had fought the battle through its most difficult years, hauled down his flag as Commander-in-Chief Western Approaches and left to become head of the British Naval Mission in Washington, a key appointment involving liaison at the highest level. His replacement was the redoubtable Admiral Sir Max Horton. As a boy, Horton had lived with his parents at Betws-y-Coed, and he had gone to school in nearby Llanrwst. As a young officer commanding the submarine *E9* during World War 1 he had sunk the German cruiser *Hela,* initiating the tradition in the British submarine service of flying the Jolly Roger on return from a successful mission. He had then moved into the Baltic where, operating from Russian bases, he had damaged a second cruiser, the *Prinz Adalbert,* and sunk three destroyers, two transports and several merchant ships. The outbreak of World War II had found him in command of the Reserve Fleet and he had subsequently commanded the Northern Patrol for several months before becoming Flag Officer Submarines, in which capacity he had proposed the construction of the midget submarine. His appointment as Commander-in-Chief Western Approaches, therefore, was that of the poacher turned gamekeeper.

Horton's temperament has been compared to Montgomery's. He was a loner and a single-minded professional, devoting 100 per cent effort to the task in hand and demanding the same of his subordinates, who were constantly required to ask themselves, 'Have I done my best?' If they had not - and he seemed to have an uncanny gift of omniscience - they could expect to feel the full weight of his fury. At sea his junior officers called him 'Der Fuhrer,' and in Liverpool the large staff of HQ Western Approaches referred to him as a right bastard, on his better days. A hard-driving taskmaster, he was not inclined to praise a man for doing the job he was paid to do, but he would reward exceptional effort and, because such occasions were rare, they were valued the more.

Tyrant in many ways though he might have been, Horton had no objection to being proved wrong, although it took an individual of singular courage to stand up to him. Shortly after taking command, he dropped in on the tactical anti-submarine warfare school established in a hut on Exchange Flags by Captain Gilbert Roberts in February 1942. Roberts's task was to train escort commanders in the tactics of defence against and counter-attack on enemy submarines, with heavy emphasis on team-work between vessels. Each captain worked in his own cubicle, seeing and hearing only as much of the battle as he would on his own bridge, without recourse to the main exercise plot, and in this way learned to co-ordinate his response with others in the simulated escort group, with the minimum of delay. Roberts explained the workings of the school to the Admiral who, to satisfy himself that neither time nor resources were being wasted, caused some consternation by announcing that he was enrolling for a week. At the end of this Roberts, with due deference to Horton's reputation as a submarine ace, asked him to play the part of the U-boat. A lengthy exercise ensued, following which Horton admitted that the escort had foiled his every attempt to get at the convoy, nodded approvingly, and left. Honour was satisfied, and no one felt inclined to tell the Admiral that he had been sunk three times in the process!

The Battle of the Atlantic reached its climax under Horton. The first three months of 1943 were disastrous for the Allies, 203,000 tons of shipping being sunk by U-boats in January, 359,000 tons in February and 627,000 tons in March. This was twice the rate of merchant-ship construction, while for every U-boat sunk two more were launched. From this point onwards, however, the balance began to tilt slowly but irrevocably against the Germans. Air-to-surface vessel radar and Leigh lights enabled coastal command aircraft to detect and kill surfaced U-boats at night, when they came up to charge their batteries, and the arrival of the Liberator long-range bomber closed the air cover gap which had existed in mid-Atlantic. In addition, the number of escort vessels had now increased to the point at which the Allied navies were able to commit hunter-killer support groups, often containing an escort carrier, the sole purpose of which was the destruction of submarines. In May forty-one U-boats were sunk, making a total of 114 for the first five months of the year. By July the number of U-boats had begun to decline while, for the first time in the war, the tonnage of Allied merchant shipping launched exceeded losses. Privately, Doenitz accepted that the battle was lost, but he refused to give up.

U-boats were fitted with the schnorkel, which enabled them to run submerged while charging their batteries, and their anti-aircraft armament was augmented. Yet, despite these measures, their losses continued to mount while the number of boats they sank each month was often trivial and only once exceeded 100,000 tons for the rest of the war.

One officer whose name remains permanently associated with the bitter struggle at sea, and with Liverpool, was Captain Frederic John Walker. An anti-submarine warfare specialist, Walker had commanded the 36th Escort Group earlier in the war and fought a series of fierce and successful actions along the Gibraltar and Arctic convoy routes. He came to Liverpool as Captain (D) in the autumn of 1942 and the following spring was appointed commander of the 2nd Support Group, consisting of Modified Black Swan Class sloops, operating out of the port.

Like Horton, Walker pushed himself and his team very hard, but his style of leadership was different. He possessed technical mastery of his subject and was able to communicate his own undoubted joy of battle, often with grimly humorous asides: 'Come over here and look at the mess you've made,' he once signalled to one of his sloops which had destroyed a U-boat with a single pattern of depth charges. The hallmark of his tactics was relentless pursuit; once a submarine contact was obtained, his group harried and hunted the unfortunate U-boat to destruction. Driven by ferocious energy, Walker's tall frame remained spare and his features were aged beyond their years by the strain of command.

On 29 January 1944 the 2nd Support Group, consisting of Walker's *Starling, Wild Goose* (Lt-Commander D.E.G Wemyss), *Woodpecker* (Lt-Commander H.L. Pryse), *Kite* (Lt-Commander W.RF. Seagrave) and *Magpie* (LtCommander R.S. Abrams), left Liverpool with a westward-bound convoy. Doenitz had meanwhile assembled no less than twenty-two U-boats for a concentrated attack on Allied shipping in the knowledge that eight convoys, inward and outward bound, would shortly be passing through the same area of sea to the west of Ireland. For his part, Horton, forewarned of enemy movements by the Ultra intercept service, was able to deploy four escort groups and three escort carriers, supported by Coastal Command aircraft flying from Northern Ireland. The battle lasted for twenty days and ended with the complete rout of the U-boats, eleven of which were sunk, six by the 2nd Support Group. Walker's last victim, *U-264,* was forced to the surface with depth charges and then engaged with gunfire before she was abandoned by her crew and sank. She was of more than usual interest as she was the first U-boat to be fitted with a schnorkel, regarding which her survivors provided much useful information.

In return the Germans only managed to sink one merchant vessel, straggling behind her convoy. During the final phase of the battle *Woodpecker's* stern was blown off by an acoustic torpedo, miraculously without loss of life or serious injury. *Kite,* having expended her munitions, had been ordered home, but the rest of the group took *Woodpecker* in tow until a tug appeared; sadly, she was overwhelmed by heavy weather off the Scillies and went down. The loss was softened by a signal from Admiral Horton informing Walker that in recognition of the group's remarkable victory it would be cheered into harbour.

It was the greatest naval occasion in the Mersey's history. Early on the morning of 25 February a huge crowd began congregating around the river entrance to Gladstone Dock. It consisted of the crews of every escort vessel in port, the entire ship's company of the battleship HMS *King George V,* berthed nearby, a Royal Marine band, staff officers, WRNS, wives and families, military police to escort the prisoners, merchant seamen and dock workers. Two special flag hoists had been run up by the base commander, Captain N.G. Brewer, himself a veteran of the Atlantic battles. The first read: 'To Second Support Group - Wonderful Achievement - Congratulations.' The second, less formal, quoted the famous whisky slogan: 'Johnny Walker Still Going Strong.'

The First Lord of the Admiralty, Mr A.V. Alexander, and Admiral Horton had already left aboard a corvette to meet the group near the Bar. And suddenly, at about 0730, there they were. Three little ships, as spick and span as their first lieutenants' wash-and-brush-up parties could make them, pushing through the morning mist and up the channel in line-ahead, *Starling* leading, followed by *Wild Goose* and *Magpie*. Aboard the corvette signal lamps flashed greetings to each as they passed. As soon as they were sighted entering the river every vessel in port sounded its welcome, the deep-throated bellow of merchant fog-horns competing with the whoop-whoopwhoop of warship sirens. There was a moment of comparative quiet as they turned left in succession to enter the lock and during this the strains of *Starling's* own theme song, the old shanty 'Down Among the Dead Men', floated across the water from her loudspeakers. Brewer called for three cheers as each vessel entered and Walker, smiling broadly, acknowledged with a formal salute from his bridge. Three cheers were nothing like enough for the crowd. They roared on and on, joined by the crews of merchant ships lining their rails. The WRNS yelled and threw their caps in the air (Wemyss thought they made as much noise as all the rest put together) and even the military police briefly abandoned their dignity. Loudhailers crackled congratulations across the dock while the sloops berthed, accompanied by 'Blaze Away', played full blast over the tannoys of an American ship. One of the group's mascots, a puppy named Steaker because of his fondness for beefsteak, fell into the dock in his eagerness for shore leave, but was deftly fished out with a sling, provoking yet more cheers. For Walker's crews, two-fifths of whom came from Merseyside, it was the homecoming of a lifetime, enlivened by banter with familiar faces ashore.

After spending a few private moments with his wife and daughter aboard *Starling,* Walker was surrounded by British, American, Norwegian and Greek naval officers wishing to offer their congratulations. Simultaneously, the captive crew of *U-264* were brought ashore. They had the submariner's pallor and they wore their hair long, brushed back from the forehead in the German manner. Some retained items of uniform, but most appeared to have been dressed from the sloops' slop chests. They were marched off, clutching their bundles of belongings, somehow small and grubby amid the jeers and almost physical dislike of the crowd. This item of business over, Walker's crews paraded to receive the personal thanks of the First Lord, who made an excellent speech and then ordered the splicing of the main brace.

Walker, already a Companion of the Order of the Bath and the holder of the Distinguished Service Order with two bars, was awarded a third bar to the latter and granted two years' seniority. He led several more patrols during which he destroyed another three U-boats, bringing his total to twenty. On return from his last patrol he was clearly tired and suddenly became ill. Two days later, on 9 July, he died in a Liverpool hospital, aged forty-eight. The immediate cause was a stroke but he had, quite simply, worked himself to death. He was accorded a public funeral at Liverpool Cathedral during which Admiral Horton paid a poignant tribute, revealing a rare glimpse of his own inner feelings. 'Not dust, nor the light weight of a stone, but all the sea of the Western Approaches shall be his tomb.' Walker was too great a seaman to be buried ashore. And so, for the second time that year, the Mersey witnessed a naval occasion. Escorted by eight captains, the gun carriage carrying the coffin was pulled to the Landing Stage by bluejackets and there placed aboard the destroyer HMS *Hesperus*. A Gibraltar-bound convoy was departing and a convoy from the United States was arriving and, as *Hesperus* passed through towards the open sea, the escorts manned ship and dipped their ensigns in silent respect.

Doenitz was developing a new, and extremely efficient, generation of U-boats, but the loss of his bases in France effectively prevented him reimposing a stranglehold on British shipping. On the other hand, the Third Reich still possessed the power to hurt the United Kingdom with its V-1 and V-2 rocket weapons. Liverpool lay beyond their range, although one freak did land near Ellesmere Port. London and the South East, however, sustained heavy casualties and damage until the Allied armies overran the launching sites, and Liverpool absorbed a number of homeless families.

The end was now in sight. During 1944 the German army in Normandy had been destroyed; France and Belgium had been liberated and the Allies had reached the frontier of Germany itself; in Italy, the formidable defences of the Gothic Line had been stormed; the Soviet Army was steamrollering its way across Poland and the Balkans; in Burma a crushing defeat had been inflicted on the Japanese at Imphal; and in the Pacific the Americans were closing in steadily on the Japanese home islands.

Yet more victories followed in the first months of 1945. The Japanese army group in Burma, out-thought and out-fought by General Slim's Fourteenth Army, was destroyed on the banks of the Irrawaddy; on the Western Front the Allies crossed the Rhine while in the East the Russians encircled Berlin; and in Italy the last German defence line was overrun and the enemy was in full retreat.

It was in Italy that the first major surrender took place on 29 April to be effective from noon on 2 May. Hitler had committed suicide on 30 April, appointing Doenitz his successor, and on 4 May the latter despatched a delegation to Field Marshal Montgomery's headquarters on Luneburg Heath, formally surrendering all German forces in North West Europe, the surrender to be effective from 0800 on 5 May. The war in Europe was over, although the enemy troops in southern Germany did not surrender until 6 May and formal ratification still had to take place.

In Liverpool there was keen competition between the newspapers to be first on the street with the news, since everyone would want a souvenir of the great day. The race was won handsomely by the *Liverpool Evening Express,* the editor of which, Mark Trench, had been preparing his Victory Issue for several weeks. It contained a summary of the war, constantly updated as campaigns drew to their conclusion; the front page was reserved for the time, date, place and circumstances of the enemy surrender, and this was completed in suitably bold type as the news came in.

The official end to hostilities in Europe was declared on 8 May, subsequently known as VE Day. Suddenly, the city was festooned with flags, flying from poles, draped from every house and strung across streets. Fog-horns blared from ships in the river, contrasting with the shrill, sustained whistles of railway locomotives. The church bells, silent for almost six years during which they could not be rung save in the event of invasion, filled the air with the welcome clamour of their clanging. Some of the peals may have sounded a little ragged because the regular bellringers were away, but their substitutes made up in enthusiasm what they lacked in expertise; one clergyman at least, forgetting to release his rope, enjoyed a short but exciting flight in the direction of his own belfry. It was a fine day and everyone converged instinctively on the city centre. My family thought that the best place to see the fun was from the top of a tram, but it became immovably stuck in a dense crowd in Lime Street, and remained so for an hour. Nobody minded, for below there was a moving sea of happy, flag-waving people, carried along on a tide of relief, singing, dancing, and hugging, overcome with the joy of it all. Impromptu street parties were organized at which almost forgotten luxury tinned foods, jealously hoarded for this very purpose, were eagerly consumed. That night, streets blazed with unaccustomed lights as the hated blackout material was torn down. Celebration bonfires were lit on bombsites, contrary to the wish of the authorities, but the police turned a blind eye; nor were the latter inclined to enforce the licensing laws as one pub after another was drunk dry. The following Sunday the churches held services of thanksgiving and many were full to the doors.

At sea, U-boats were surfacing to surrender to the nearest Allied warship. On 17 May *U-532* was brought into Gladstone Dock. She was a submarine freighter and had been on passage home from Japan with a cargo of raw materials including 110 tons of tin, plus rubber, molybdenum and wolfram. Her capture confirmed the desperate straits to which the blockaded German war industry had been reduced and provided a stark contrast with the wealth of materials pouring through Liverpool. The following month a fighting boat, *U-1023,* was opened to public view in Canning Dock and subsequently in Morpeth Dock, Birkenhead. No charge was made, although a collection was taken in aid of King George's Fund for Sailors. The interior of the submarine seemed impossibly cramped and retained an unpleasant odour compounded of cooking, urine, sweat and machinery.

Meanwhile, the war with Japan continued. The enemy's position was hopeless but everyone knew that the Japanese fought to the death and there was concern that they would inflict heavy casualties before they were finally overwhelmed. In the event, the war ended with dramatic suddenness. On 6 August an atomic bomb was dropped on Hiroshima; on 8 August the Soviet Union declared war on Japan and launched a massive invasion of Manchuria; on 9 August a second atomic bomb was dropped on Nagasaki. The fact that more people had died in incendiary raids on Japanese cities than in either of the atomic bomb explosions could not conceal the horrific nature of the latter. On 10 August the Japanese announced that they were willing to talk and four days later they agreed to surrender unconditionally.

In Liverpool VJ Day, 15 August, was celebrated in much the same way as VE Day. The official celebrations lasted from 22 to 30 September. The Corporation allocated £20,000 and was at pains to ensure that no one was left out. Special provision was made for members of the armed services stationed locally, the Merchant Navy, repatriated prisoners of war, disabled ex-servicemen, the police, NFS, Civil Defence services, war widows and dependent parents - a total of 17,700. Of these, 4,800 were entertained on two nights at the Empire Theatre, 5,000 on one night at the Stadium, 2,000 went dancing at the Grafton Rooms on two nights, 1,000 attended a concert at the Philharmonic Hall, and for the remainder entertainment was provided on two or three nights at the Ocean Club, the Gordon Smith Institute for Seamen, the Sailors' Home, the Mersey Mission to Seamen, the Apostleship of the Sea and the Allied Centre. The city's 126,300 schoolchildren had tea parties in their schools, followed by some form of entertainment, the arrangements being left to head teachers, who were allowed 1/- per head. At the municipal hospitals there were dances for the day and night staffs, and parties for the patients; the 1,400 children in hospital also received toys. Those in receipt of public assistance were granted an additional 3/- per adult and 2/- per child. The Liverpool Aged Poor Dinner and Relief Fund hired a marquee in which 2,000 people aged seventy and over were provided with dinner and a surprise parcel. Tea and concerts were arranged by the Council of Social Service for 1,500 residents of charitable homes, and by the Home Teaching Society for 1,600 blind persons. The Deaf and Dumb Benevolent Society also arranged tea, followed by an outing, for 1,000 of its members.

The Corporation itself held a reception for the large Liverpool Consular Corps in the Town Hall, which was also the scene of a Victory Ball attended by councillors, local dignitaries and senior officers of the services. For everyone, bands played at the Church Street car park, on St George's Hall Plateau, which was also used for open-air dancing on fine evenings, and in the parks, some of which housed travelling fun fairs. It had been hoped to stage a firework display, but the manufacturers were still engaged in more serious business. On the other hand, a successful attempt to simulate the return of peaceful affluence was made by floodlighting the Town Hall, St George's Hall, the Wellington Column and the Steble Fountain, and by erecting decorations and special illuminations in Lime Street. A very pleasant effect was achieved by lighting Sefton Park Lake, on which boating was permitted until midnight. Most spectacular of all was the reappearance of the Illuminated Tram, not seen since the Coronation, a wonderful machine glowing with thousands of coloured electric bulbs, which toured the city with a band playing on the open upper deck.

The festivities ended with a Victory parade held during the afternoon of Sunday 30 September. The various contingents fell in near the University and then marched down Mount Pleasant and through the city centre. Crowds had turned out to watch, but they were mostly silent and there was little cheering or clapping. This was quite uncharacteristic of Liverpool people and has puzzled me ever since. Perhaps it was a reflective reaction to all that had gone before, and perhaps it was a recognition that the parade marked the end of an era in which we had all shared equally. The war, with its horrors, dangers, sense of purpose and comradeship we had learned to understand and live with; the peace which lay ahead was an unknown quantity. Thus, in Liverpool the Second World War ended as it had begun, quietly on a Sunday.

Headquarters Western Approaches Command had closed down on 15 August and Horton retired from the Royal Navy in November. Liverpool had come to regard him as one of its own and in 1946 the Corporation conferred on him the Honorary Freedom of the City, an honour which he said was 'shared and earned by every man Jack and woman Jill' under his command. At the ceremony itself he added:

> Whilst for nearly six years the swaying battle in the North Atlantic went on, the whole population of this city and port of Liverpool were working for victory at the docks, at the yards, or in the factories, warehouses and shops. Liverpool was the principal port of the United Kingdom during the war. The unceasing effort of its inhabitants with their stern resolve to keep going in every adversity was admirable to observe. They set an example which withstood every bitter test the Nazi could provide.
>
> It is small wonder then that I am very moved today by the great honour your city has thought fit to confer on me. The beautiful casket you have given me with its symbolic design will ever recall great days and highly charged moments together with poignant memories of those gallant men who paid the price of victory.

> I thank you for this day, not only on my own behalf, but on behalf of all who served under me in one of history's longest and most bitterly contested battles at sea - the nerve centre of which was situated in your great city of Liverpool.

Admiral Sir Max Horton died in July 1951 and was cremated in London. On 7 August his ashes were brought to Liverpool for interment in the south-east transept of Liverpool Cathedral. Watched by thousands, standing ten deep in places, the gun carriage was escorted on its journey from St George's Hall Plateau by a Royal Marine band and 500 officers and ratings. It was the final postscript to great events.

Since then, the generations have passed, the scars have healed and much has changed. It is difficult now for the young to imagine that Liverpool was once the Second City of Empire or that the survival of the United Kingdom once depended upon the port. The incessant passage of ships on the river, the rumbling Overhead Railway, the noisy trams and the clatter of horse-drawn carts on the Dock Road have all gone, vanished into memory like the last sparks of the victory bonfires. Today, the sights and sounds are different. But the people remain.

Bibilography

Allen, Professor Jack, 'Experiments Made at Manchester University Concerning Anti-Aircraft Gun Towers Erected in Liverpool Bay', pp.120-131 in Vol. 3 of The *Civil Engineer in War* (Institution of Civil Engineers, 1947)

Argyle, Christopher J., 'The Liverpool Blitz - German Air Raids on Merseyside, August 1940 to May 1941', articles in *Air Pictorial* magazine, 1975

Buckley, T.J., *Port at War* (Mersey Docks & Harbour Board, 1946)

Chandler, George, *Four Centuries of Banking* (Batsford, 1964)

Collier, Basil, *The Defence of the United Kingdom* (HMSO, 1954)

Foreman, John, *Battle of Britain - The Forgotten Months* (Air Research Publications, 1988)

Jarvis, Adrian, *Docks of the Mersey* (Ian Allan in association with the National Museums and Galleries on Merseyside, 1988)

Jones, Ron, *The American Connection - The Story of Liverpool's Links with America from Christopher Colombus to the Beatles* (private publication, 1986)

Joyce, J., *Roads, Rails & Ferries of Liverpool 1900-1950* (Ian Allan,1983)

Lane, Tony, *Liverpool - Gateway of Empire* (Lawrence & Wishart, 1987)

Leslie, S.C., and others, *Bombers over Merseyside (Liverpool Daily Post and Echo* Ltd, reprinted by Scouse Press, 1983)

Maurice-Jones, Colonel K.W., *The History of Coastal*

Artillery in the British Army (Royal Artillery Institution, 1959)
Mountfield, S., *Western Gateway* (Mersey Docks & Harbour Board)
Nash, George C., *The LMS at War* (London Midland and Scottish Railway Company)
Perrett, Bryan, and Hogg, Ian, *Encyclopedia of the Second World War* (Longman, 1989)
Pile, General Sir Frederick, *Ack-Ack* (Harrap,1949)
Posford, John Albert, *'The Construction of Britain's Sea Forts,'* pp. 132 - 180 in Vol. 3 of *The Civil Engineer in War* (Institution of Civil Engineers, 1947)
Price, Alfred, *Blitz on Britain* (Ian Allan,1972)
——'Liverpool Blitz' in *War Monthly* magazine, no. 33, 1976
Robertson, John D., *Fire Fighters of Merseyside Past and Present* (Merseyside Fire Brigade)
Slader, John, *The Red Duster at War - A History of the Merchant Navy During the Second World War* (William Kimber,1988)
Smith, David J., *Action Stations 3 - Military Airfields of Wales and the North West* (Patrick Stephens, 1981)
Vat, Dan van der, *The Atlantic Campaign - The Great Struggle at Sea 1939-1945* (Hodder & Stoughton, 1988)
Wakefield, K., *The First Pathfinders* (William Kimber, 1981)
Wemyss, Commander *D.E.G., Relentless Pursuit* (William Kimber, 1955)
Whale, Derek M., *The Liners of Liverpool, Parts I & II* (Countyvise, 1986/87)
Whittington-Egan, Richard, *The Great Liverpool Blitz* (Gallery Press, 1987)
Whitworth, Rodney, *Merseyside at War - A Day-by-Day Diary of the 1940-1941 Bombing* (Scouse Press, 1988)
Wood, Tony, and Gunston, Bill, *Hitler's Luftwaffe* (Salamander, 1981)

Index